Corporate Social Responsibility and Development in Pakistan

Corporate Social Responsibility (CSR) has not only become an important concept for corporate organizations but also civil society, community, state and the multilateral and bilateral development agencies. It has acquired great significance in the aftermath of the global financial crisis of 2008, not only in the advanced, but also in emerging economies. In contemporary Pakistan problems of poverty, unemployment, illiteracy, and human rights violations are frequent. These problems cannot be dealt with by the state and civil society alone and call for corporate involvement.

Backed by rich empirical data, based on extensive fieldwork and complemented with the official data sources, this book offers a detailed analysis of the socially responsible corporate policies and practices of companies operating in the emerging economy of Pakistan. Employing qualitative and quantitative research methods, it examines the sensitivity of companies in Pakistan to CSR measured in terms of their policies and perceptions about CRS, their CSR development activities, perceptions about development Non-Governmental Organisations, and channels and forms of support for development projects (both monetary and non-monetary).

Filling a significant gap in our understanding of an important part of contemporary Pakistan's development and the outlook of companies towards CSR, the book will be of interest to policymakers and scholars working in the fields of Development Studies, Business Studies and Asian Studies.

Nadeem Malik is the Director of Master of Development Studies Program, at the University of Melbourne, Australia. His research interests include governance and decentralization, civil society, corporate social responsibility and development. He is the author of *Citizens and Governance in Pakistan: the analysis of people's voice.*

Routledge Contemporary South Asia Series

Corporate Social Responsibility and Development in Pakistan

Nadeem Malik

Routledge
Taylor & Francis Group

LONDON AND NEW YORK

First published 2015
by Routledge
2 Park Square, Milton Park, Abingdon, Oxon OX14 4RN

and by Routledge
711 Third Avenue, New York, NY 10017

Routledge is an imprint of the Taylor & Francis Group, an informa business

British Library Cataloguing in Publication Data
A catalogue record for this book is available from the British Library

Library of Congress Cataloging in Publication Data
Malik, Nadeem, 1962- author.
Corporate social responsibility and development in Pakistan /
Nadeem Malik.
    pages ; cm. -- (Routledge contemporary South Asia series ; 87)
1. Social responsibility of business--Pakistan. 2. Corporations--Social
aspects--Pakistan. 3. Economic development--Pakistan. 4. Pakistan--
Economic conditions. I. Title. II. Series: Routledge contemporary South
Asia series ; 87.
    HD60.5.P18M35 2015
    338.95491--dc23
        2014008110

ISBN: 978-0-415-70911-8 (hbk)
ISBN: 978-1-315-88572-8 (ebk)

Typeset in Times New Roman
by Taylor & Francis Books

MIX
Paper from
responsible sources
FSC
www.fsc.org   FSC® C013604

Printed and bound by CPI Group (UK) Ltd, Croydon, CR0 4YY

Contents

List of Illustrations

Tables

Figures

Boxes

Acknowledgements

Many people have helped me in conducting this research and writing this book. First, I am indebted to Dr Fouzia Saeed, who was Actionaid Pakistan's Country Director and sponsored my preliminary research on this topic and my participation in CSR conference in New Delhi, organized by Actionaid India in 2001. Next, I wish to thank Professor Shalendra Sharma from the University of San Francisco who encouraged me to conduct my recent research for this book.

I also owe a great deal of gratitude to Mr. Ayyaz Kiani, Director of Devnet Pakistan, who helped identify important secondary data and provided field researchers for this study in Pakistan. I am also thankful to Bryonny Goodwin, and Sara Malik, from the University of Melbourne who read my draft and made valuable comments. Mr. Waseem Malik, a leading figure in textiles trade, introduced me to a number of important corporate leaders in Pakistan, also deserves my thanks.

Finally, I offer my thanks to a number CEOs and other officials of companies in various cities in Pakistan, who provided me guidance and valuable time for interviews and informal conversations.

1 Introduction

After the decolonization of developing countries in Asia, Africa and Latin America, development became an international concern. It is generally acknowledged that the genesis of development lies in President Truman's concept of a 'fair deal' for the entire world announced in his 1949 speech. While mentioning the misery experienced by people because of poverty and disease, one of the major rationales provided by Truman was that 'their poverty is a handicap and a threat both to them and to more prosperous areas' (Truman 1949, as cited in Escobar 1995: 3).

During the colonial period, overcoming poverty was not an international concern. In this connection Escobar (1995: 22) notes that:

> Poverty on a global scale was a discovery of the post-World War II period. As Sachs (1990) and Rehnema (1991) have maintained, the conceptions and treatment of poverty were quite different before 1940. In colonial times the concern with poverty was conditioned by the belief that even if the 'natives' could be somewhat enlightened by the presence of the colonizer, not much could be done about their poverty because their economic development was pointless

During the colonial period, it was possible for the developed part of the world to progress at the expense of the underdeveloped part. However, once countries in the developing world achieved independence and sovereignty accompanied by increasing interconnectedness around the world through information technology, trade and finance, it was no longer possible for one part of the world to develop at the expense of the other. Therefore, when Truman referred to world poverty as a threat to both prosperous and poor countries, he was signaling the fact that in order to maintain the living standards of people in developed countries, something had to be done to deal with poverty in developing countries. This was not possible without development to increase the purchasing power of people living in developing countries that represented major markets for the products of the developed world.

It is appalling, however, that amidst the material comfort and unprecedented prosperity of the twenty-first century, more than a billion people still live in miserably abject conditions. Poverty is still a pressing issue for international financial institutions such as the World Bank and the IMF, and Ravallion & Chen (2009: 22) conclude that poverty is 'more pervasive' than previously thought. Estimates placed 1.4 billion people below the $1.25-a-day international poverty line in 2005, an 8 per cent jump from 1993 estimates that classified only 17 per cent of the developing world's population as poor (Ravallion & Chen 2009: 22).

Traditionally, governments and international donors have led development efforts. Multilateral and bilateral aid, aid for food and humanitarian assistance, trade policies, inter-governmental loans and charity are considered essential for mitigating poverty. However, such instruments have not solved the problem of the global poor (Collier 2007), allowing the entry of businesses into the arena of development.

Thus, development has become an important concept not only for government, civil society and the multilateral and bilateral development agencies but also for the business sector. Increased globalization accompanied by the increasing influence of corporate organizations has put more pressure on business corporations to be socially responsible (Warden 2007) and contribute to the development of poor communities. Moreover, 'the 1980s saw a significant shift away from state intervention in both developed and developing countries' (Jenkins 2005: 527), emphasizing the need for the corporate sector to play a significant role in development, traditionally the responsibility of the state. It is generally believed that, with the kind of resources and global reach corporations have today, they can play a significant role in achieving the goal of social and economic development. International development agencies have put forward an agenda for cross-sector partnerships between the state, civil society and the market and corporate social responsibility (CSR) has emerged as one of many responses to alleviating poverty and underdevelopment alongside the concepts of social entrepreneurship, bottom of the pyramid (BoP) schemes (Prahalad 2005), and 'creative capitalism' (Kinsley, 2008).

However, over the last decades corporate scandals have invited increasing criticism of firms (Basu & Palazzo 2008). Oil and mining companies especially have been the target of criticism (see e.g. Frynas & Wood 2001). Critics, in 'particular from the NGO community, denounce the hypocrisy of a practice that they view as mere corporate PR exercises, with no capacity, willingness or even prospects to influence the structural determinants of underdevelopment, un-sustainability and injustice' (Amalric *et al.* 2004: 3). All this means that the legitimacy of corporate operations has been increasingly questioned, with pressure put on companies to renew their 'social license to operate' (Castello & Lozano 2011) through responsible business practices and contributing to communities through development.

Simultaneously, international agencies have taken the initiative to pressure companies to act in socially responsible ways. The UN Global Compact is the best known of these initiatives. It has incorporated over 10,000 corporate participants and other stakeholders from over 130 countries. It is also the largest voluntary corporate responsibility initiative in the world (UNGC 2012). The UN Global Compact asks companies to support and enact a set of core values in the areas of human rights, labour standards, the environment and anti-corruption. It has articulated ten core principles in the following areas (see Box 1.1).

Box 1.1 UN Global Compact: ten principles

Human rights

Principle 1: Business should support and respect the protection of internationally proclaimed human rights; and
   Principle 2: make sure that they are not complicit in human rights abuse.

Labour

Principle 3: Business should uphold the freedom of association and the effective recognition of the right to collective bargaining;
   Principle 4: the elimination of all forms of forced and compulsory labour;
   Principle 5: the effective abolition of child labour; and
   Principle 6: the elimination of discrimination in respect of employment and occupation.

Environment

Principle 7: Business should support a precautionary approach to environmental challenges;
   Principle 8: undertake initiatives to promote greater environmental responsibility; and
   Principle 9: encourage the development and diffusion of environmentally friendly technologies.

Anti-corruption

Principle 10: Business should work against corruption in all its forms, including extortion and bribery.
   UNGC (www.unglobalcompact.org/abouttheGC/TheTenPrinciples/index.html)

The major concern has been to reform the ways companies treat their stakeholders (clients, employees, investors, and the local communities where they operate) 'and/or the impact of its activities on society at large, without having recourse to direct regulation, and with the objective of promoting social justice and sustainability' (Amalric *et al.* 2004: 1).

This background of increasing demands from a broad range of stakeholders including international agencies has resulted in heightened pressure on companies to conduct their business in a socially responsible manner. Yet over the last decade we have also seen a shift from an overly critical approach to positive engagement between companies and their stakeholders. In Europe:

> business organizations and their stakeholders are taking collaborative actions for debating and creating CSR policies and strategies to achieve a competitive advantage at a national stage and to move towards the next wave of responsible competitiveness, which is innovation, sustainability and future focus.
>
> (Waheed 2005: 3)

Most countries in the Asia Pacific are also going through the so-called second wave of CSR, which is efficiency-centered and market-focused (Waheed 2005: 3). The companies are expected to engage in culturally and socially sensitive development work in a participatory manner, recognizing and addressing power imbalances.

On the other hand, the development sector is facing a new landscape in regard to resource mobilization for development in the face of diminishing foreign aid. The decline of foreign aid has been well entrenched globally since 1999 (Edwards *et al.* 1999: 6). Official development aid (ODA) targets have also not been achieved. These targets are set as a percentage of annual gross national income (GNI) of each donor country within the OECD (Organization for Economic Co-operation and Development). In 1970, the UN had set the target of 0.7 per cent of GNI for ODA, but the DAC (OECD Development Assistance Committee) donors achieved only 0.29 per cent of GNI in 2012 (DI 2012). According to Development Initiatives (DI) (2012: 59), in 2011 the net ODA from DAC donors fell 2.2 per cent in real terms (US$2.9 billion), followed by a further fall of 23.9 per cent (US$5.2 billion). In 2012, the total ODA funding of DAC members was US$128 billion, of which US$15.36 billion (12 per cent) went to NGOs. Compared to 2003, when NGOs received US$15.5 billion (OECD 2007, as cited in Dreher *et al.* 2007: 3), there is a fall of US$0.14 billion in 2012. The funding for NGOs, therefore, remains stagnant and the competition for resources has become a major characteristic of the NGO sector the world over (Edwards *et al.* 1999).

Moreover, in the absence of reliable data regarding the financing of Southern NGOs, it is uncertain what percentage of funds are channeled through these NGOs, as a substantial share of official funding goes to Northern NGOs. For example, from 2007 to 2011 NGOs (mainly INGOs) together contributed over US$20 billion to humanitarian assistance from private sources while also channeling US$14.4 billion from official donor sources (Morton 2013: 334).

In addition, due to the commercialization of aid, consulting companies within DAC countries consume a substantial amount of aid. In particular, the practice of contracting out technical assistance to advisers and experts has been criticized as making inadequate use of recipient countries' infrastructures and contravening the spirit of partnership, as well as being an inefficient and ineffective way to spend money. Notably, current practices also ultimately act as a form of 'boomerang aid', with over 50 per cent return via salaries for contractors (AidWatch 2005). One such example is Australian aid. The Australian National Audit Office (ANAO 2009) found that 46 per cent of AusAID's budget is designated for 'technical assistance', which is then contracted out.

Several scholars have warned about the consequences of declining development aid for NGOs, particularly Southern NGOs. As early as 2000, Fowler (2000: 589) stressed that non-governmental development organizations (NGDOs) should consider planning their work by searching alternative sources of local funding in the beyond-aid scenario in the twenty-first century. He argued that the:

> 'Practical reason why NGDOs must consider life in a beyond-aid scenario results from the decreasing volume and redistribution of aid finance. While amounting to US$51.5 billion in 1998, since 1991 the real value of aid from the North has dropped by some 21 per cent' (DI 1999). What you see in such figures is not what you get as aid in the South. However, even definitional sleights of hand cannot obscure the fact that donor countries have become both richer and meaner. Per capita incomes of OECD countries grew from an average of $11,575 in 1960 to $27, 789 in 1997, i.e. by 140 per cent. In the same period per capita aid from OECD countries grew from $47 to $59, i.e. by 25 per cent (DI 1999).
>
> (Fowler 2000: 590)

In the same vein, Aldaba *et al.* (2000) also emphasize the beyond-aid scenario for the NGO community. Malhotra (2000) goes even further than this, arguing that a future without aid would be a positive development if this was an outcome of the transition of the developing world from its present condition of poverty to the total alleviation of that poverty. After all, he argued, 'conceptually, aid has always been viewed as a transitionary but necessary evil until poverty is removed. It is clearly not desirable as a permanent state of affairs!' (Malhotra 2000: 656).

What is unfortunate according to Malhotra (2000: 656) is that the future without aid that we need to contemplate is not coming about due to a decline in poverty but because rich industrialized countries have chosen to reduce concessionary assistance to developing countries in favour of private capital flows.

In view of the declining foreign funding scenario, authors such as Aldaba *et al.* (2000) and Holloway (2001) have suggested alternative strategies for raising local resources for the sustainability of NGO projects in the long run. Both have made a case for local resource mobilization. Aldaba *et al.* (2000) emphasize that the concept of sustainability should not be defined in terms of the possession of mere monetary resources. Sustainability ultimately depends on the nature of the relationship between NGOs and their surroundings. In other words, sustainability is dependent on the support of people who live in the society NGOs work in. If local constituencies support NGOs, getting financial and other kinds of support is not difficult.

As part of local resources mobilization, one of the final alternatives to foreign funding suggested by Aldaba *et al.* (2000) is soliciting support from the corporate sector. Citing Velasco (1995) regarding the Philippines they mention that 'various studies have yielded the following total resources from corporations and local foundations—US$12.35 million in 1993, $12.81 and as high as $31.41 million in 1994' (Aldaba *et al.* 2000: 681). This also contributed to 'gradually mellowing down the antagonism that existed between NGOs and the corporate sector' (Aldaba *et al.* 2000: 681). In Central America some 13 per cent of NGOs surveyed indicated that business grants were one source of their income (Aldaba *et al.* 2000).

Apart from declining foreign aid, another major factor vis-à-vis dependence on foreign funding by development NGOs is their declining legitimacy within society. The question of NGOs' accountability and legitimacy at grassroots level due to dependence on foreign funding has been identified by several development scholars (see, for example, Mercer 2002, Fowler 1991, Bebbington 1997, Holloway 2001, Gideon 1998, Farrington and Lewis 1993). These scholars have argued that NGOs are increasingly becoming accountable to donors rather than their local constituencies. It is worrying that 'foreign aid inadvertently undermines NGOs ties to local populations, handing angry governments an opportunity for successful crackdowns' (Dupuy *et al.* 2012: 3). In 2010, for example, 'the Ethiopian government's new anti NGO law, the Charities and Societies proclamation, blocked foreign funding groups from working on Ethiopian human rights and democracy' (Dupuy *et al.* 2012: 3).

Fowler (2000) notes that foreign-funded developing countries' NGOs have become subsidy-providing intermediaries on behalf of global donors. The result is increasing dependence on outside sources, pathological institutional behaviour and financial malpractice. Such circumstances question the very legitimacy of NGOs within society. All of this occurs against the backdrop of an ever more crowded NGO sector, which is beginning to be characterized by duplication, turf wars over issues and funding, and a lack of transparency and sustainable thinking. While these projects are led by well-meaning organizations that hope to make a positive impact, many of the initiatives disempower locals, begin the cycle of complete reliance on outside sources of funding and, in fact, retard the development of an indigenous citizen resource base.

Soliciting support for welfare causes require new approaches because of ever-increasing globalized economic systems (Kshetri 2011). The recent global financial crisis was a wake-up call regarding the way inefficient economic performance with a global impact negatively influences countries that rely on foreign funding (Schultz 2009). Moreover, there is an increase in internal demands relating to the social and economic needs of citizens within industrially developed nations, which in the long run could lead to redirecting funds to the developed world and further decline in foreign funding for developing countries.

Local resource mobilization, therefore, has emerged as an important theme, and international organizations such as CIVICUS and Agha Khan Foundations have designed training programmes for NGOs in the South to mobilize local development resources.

Local resource mobilization requires the support of local people friendly to an organization's cause. Fundraising in this context is known as friends-raising. The more friends you have the more funds you can collect for a cause. When NGOs depend largely on foreign funding, they tend to cultivate friends within the donor community, paying less attention to local constituencies. Holloway (2001), therefore, while emphasizing the financial self-reliance of non-government development organizations argues that development is a political discourse. When NGOs solely depend on foreign funding, neglecting to establish local support, they provide ammunition for local dissenters within the state and outside to discredit NGOs by labeling them agents of foreign interests. Such a state of affairs further erodes their legitimacy within society.

To deal with this predicament, it is imperative to find new approaches to financing local non-government organizations. Mobilizing the vast resources of the corporate sector is a good option, achievable by enhancing CSR movement in developing countries through practical efforts and research.

In addition, while there have been efforts to establish a causal link between CSR and financial performance, there has been relatively little analysis of the nature of their partnership with development NGOs. Moreover, the researchers have focused on the incorporation of CSR issues into business practices in developed economies (Wise & Ali 2008). However, since the concept of corporate social responsibility is newer for emerging economies there is little to be found on the socially responsible corporate policies and practices of companies operating in countries such as Pakistan. This study looks at large, medium and small indigenous companies operating in Pakistan and examines the sensitivity of companies to CSR and development, which is measured in terms of their perceptions about CSR, their CSR policies and activities, perceptions about NGOs, and their channels and forms of support (both monetary and nonmonetary).

Including Chapter 1, the book is structured around nine chapters. Chapter 2 provides a history and analysis of the origins of the concepts of CSR and development. It also discusses various definitions of CSR and their evolution. It is argued that, contrary to the general belief that the major reason for the CSR movement was the pressures of consumer and solidarity movements, there were other important factors – for instance, the Cold War context that created a need for CSR to be actively promoted in the mid-twentieth century. The modern CSR construct therefore had an implicit ideological dimension. The concept of development was also developed in the mid-twentieth century as an ideological construct.

Chapter 3 provides a rationale for CSR by providing the current context of underdevelopment in Pakistan. It provides an analysis of poverty and inequality in the country, looking at income and employment shares, rural poverty, women's development and social indicators such as health, education and housing. It demonstrates that the state has failed to deliver in these areas, which calls for civil society and corporate action to contribute. Since the corporate sector generates such enormous resources, it needs to actively give something back to society.

Chapter 4 provides a historical analysis of industrial development and the corporate management culture in Pakistan. It is argued that the under-development of industry and management culture has significantly influenced the way CSR is managed in Pakistan, where religion, elitism and kinship-based social values inform CSR practices.

Chapter 5 offers an analysis of the government's role in CSR by providing examples of European and Asian countries, followed by information on Pakistan's government regulations and recent guidelines and initiatives inten-ded to enhance CSR in the country. It has yet to be seen, however, how far such initiatives bear fruit.

Chapter 6 analyzes the perceptions of the indigenous corporate sector regarding CSR in Pakistan. It demonstrates that overall, due to particular his-torical traditions of philanthropic/charity work and community life, percep-tions of CSR do not go beyond employee and community welfare, though some included paying taxes in their definition. As against welfare approaches, the modern concept of sustainable development has yet to reach the radar of most companies. The major motivation is religion.

Chapter 7 provides information about and analysis of company CSR poli-cies and practices in Pakistan. It reports that, since the idea of CSR is new in Pakistan, only 17 per cent of companies have written CSR policies. In addi-tion, CSR policies and the implementation of those policies is highly cen-tralized – in most cases, company CEOs formulate and implement them. The reasons behind the dearth of CSR policies are also analyzed. CSR activities are managed in a haphazard way and are highly disorganized. In most cases the CSR response to people's needs are demand- rather than supply-based. Welfare rather than development activities are preferred, contrasting with the way CSR is conceived in industrially advanced countries in the North.

Chapter 8 reports and analyzes the channels of support for CSR activities preferred by companies in Pakistan. A vast majority of companies prefer to channel their support directly to end beneficiaries; a small segment prefer channeling such support through intermediate professional bodies such as NGOs, and companies' own welfare organizations. Only those companies that work through intermediate bodies have CSR policy. Chapter 8 also provides information about the forms of support companies prefer. Most companies prefer monetary support. Others prefer providing support in-kind. It is demonstrated that the credibility and transparency of individuals and organizations is the most important criterion behind extending monetary as well as non-monetary support. Chapter 9 provides an overall conclusion and further reflections on research findings.

Research methodology

Study settings

This is a field-based study that examines the attitudes and behaviours of people, representing different companies, towards CSR in their working environment. Variables were neither controlled nor manipulated and no artificial settings were created for the study.

Research sample

The population studied consists of CEOs and finance directors, directors of administration and other senior officials, representing different corporate organizations (large-scale, medium-scale and small-scale indigenous companies in Pakistan). The sample frame consists of 151 sampling units i.e. N = 151.

Sampling procedure

In order to identify study respondents a stratified random sampling procedure was adopted. Around 200 companies were identified as a target sample; 151 companies committed to participate.

Separate lists of companies were developed on the basis of sources such as the list of companies developed by Lahore, Karachi, Gujranwala, Faisalabad and Sialkot chambers of commerce and industry and the Yellow Pages of Pakistan. The companies were then grouped into 14 major sectors, ensuring the representation of major industry/business sectors.

The distribution of the sample by location

As indicated in Table 1.1, companies were selected from five major industrial cities, Sialkot, Gujranwala, Lahore, Faisalabad and Karachi. Distribution-wise, 9.9 per cent of the companies in the sample were from Sialkot, 15 per cent from Gujranwala, 31.1 per cent from Lahore, 24.5 per cent from Faisalabad and 24.5 per cent from Karachi. The field study mainly focused on medium, large and small national companies, since multinational companies already have coherent corporate social policies documented in written form and getting information about their development interventions is not difficult. It was considered more important to learn the perceptions of the local

Table 1.1 Distribution of sample by location

Cities	No.	%	Valid %	Cumulative %
Sialkot	15	9.9	9.9	9.9
Gujranwala	15	9.9	9.9	19.9
Lahore	47	31.1	31.1	51
Faisalabad	37	24.5	24.5	75.5
Karachi	37	24.5	24.5	100
Total	151	100	100	

Table 1.2 Geographical area of business operations

Geographical area	No.	%
Industrial	27	17.9
Commercial	118	78.1
Residential	6	4
Total	151	100

corporate sector regarding CSR and the nature of their current involvement in development projects in Pakistan.

Geographical area of business operations

As shown in Table 1.2, 27 per cent of companies were operating in industrial areas, 78.1 per cent in commercial areas and 4 per cent in residential areas.

Companies by size

The following two parameters were adopted to determine company size:

1. Asset size
2. Size of labour force employed

Asset size

The value of assets owned by companies ranged from Rs 1 million to Rs 500 million. These were mostly medium and large national companies. Four per cent of the companies owned assets worth Rs 100 million and 4 per cent owned assets worth Rs 500 million. 24.5 per cent of companies refused to disclose their asset base. Details of companies' assets is given in Figure 1.1.

Companies by size of labour force employed

As indicated in Table 1.3, 54.3 per cent of companies had fewer than 100 employees (mostly small and medium-size companies), 27.2 per cent had

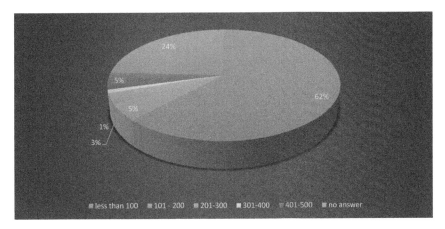

Figure 1.1 Total assets (Rs in million)

Table 1.3 Number of employees

Total number of employees	No.	%	Valid %	Cumulative %
Less than 100	82	54.3	54.3	54.3
100 to 500	41	27.2	27.2	81.5
Above 500	28	18.5	18.5	100
Total	151	100	100	

between 100 and 500 employees (medium and large companies) and 18.5 per cent had more than 500 employees (large companies operating at national and international levels).

Research tools

This was qualitative as well as quantitative research and used in-depth interviews and a survey as data collection tools. In-depth interviews were conducted in order to acquire data about the perceptions of chief executive officers and other senior officials of different companies, and a survey based on a structured questionnaire was used for an analysis of companies' perceptions of CSR, their involvement in development projects, their perceptions of NGOs, forms of support for development and the extent to which they monitor and evaluate the projects supported by them.

A pilot study was conducted with ten companies to test the questionnaire. Subsequently, changes were made and errors removed. The questionnaire was then handed over to the field researchers, who started arranging appointments with representatives of the various corporate sector organizations. In order to secure the participation of senior officials (in filling out the questionnaires and being interviewed), the field researchers made initial contact by sending letters and personally visiting the companies. A number of queries were faced by the field researchers, the most common being: what was the purpose of the study, whom will the study benefit, where will the information acquired be used, and will the company have to donate funds after participating in the survey.

After a company completed the questionnaire, in-depth interviews were conducted with the CEO or another senior official. In the event, in-depth interviews of the CEOs of all companies included in the survey were conducted. The interviews were semi-structured in nature and a complete checklist of questions was developed to act as a guide.

A two-day orientation workshop

Following the completion of the questionnaire survey and a question checklist for semi-structured in-depth interviews, a two-day workshop was conducted to familiarise the field researchers with the nature and scope of the study. The workshop included a briefing on the concept of corporate social responsibility the world over, growing trends regarding corporate accountability and citizenship and the role of the corporate sector in development. In addition, a detailed discussion was held regarding the administration of the questionnaire and avoiding personal bias when conducting interviews.

2 CSR and development

How the two concepts evolved

Though corporate social responsibility has been widely discussed during the last fifty years, the idea that business has a social obligation is much older. Ethical principles for business practices to control greed were advocated by thinkers such as Cicero in the pre-Christian period in the West in the first century and their counterparts in non-Western societies such as Chanakya Kautilya in fourth century India. Islam and the medieval Christian Church condemned certain business practices, notably usury (Blowfield & Frynas 2005: 500).

In modern times, 'the idea that business has societal obligations was evident at least as early as the nineteenth century' (Smith 2003: 1). In Britain, for example, business leaders built factory towns, such as Bourneville in 1879 and Port Sunlight in 1888 (Smith 2003: 1). These towns provided workers and their families with housing and other amenities when many parts of the newly industrialized cities were slums in the aftermath of the Industrial Revolution (Smith 2003: 1). In the United States, with the same motivation, George Pullman's town was built on the outskirts of Chicago (Smith 2003: 1).

Nevertheless, CSR has never been more prominent on the corporate agenda than it is today. Bowen (1953) is considered the father of the modern concept of corporate social responsibility. He initiated discussions about CSR, suggesting that executives should pursue 'those policies, decisions, lines of action that add objectivity and value to our society' (Bowen 1953: 6, as cited in Carroll 1999: 270). In these early writings, CSR was 'referred to more often as social responsibility (SR) than as CSR' (Carroll 1999: 269).

It is generally believed that CSR is an outcome of social pressures on corporations. Waheed (2005: 5) suggests that:

> CSR has its roots in consumer consciousness and solidarity movements in developed consumer societies that saw elements of social and environmental exploitation in the behavior of major global enterprises, whether they were mining or natural resource exploration companies or retailers sourcing consumer goods and produce from cheap labor markets in the developing world. From initial finger pointing and confrontationist strategies spearheaded by NGOs and civil rights activists to the blossoming

of a host of sustainability partnerships between these same NGOs and their erstwhile corporate foes, CSR has definitely come a long way.

This view is somewhat shared by other scholars such as Smith (2003), Blow-field & Frynas (2005) and Lee (2008). While it is pertinent, it overlooks the Cold War context that was also significant in giving birth to the CSR movement. In this connection, Spector argued that the CSR concept emerged as an ideological construct during the Cold War period, stating that:

> Cold War ideology hardened into a pervasive consensus by 1949, crossing domestic party lines while embracing both liberals and conservatives. That consensus held that Soviet communism represented more than just a threat to Western power and dominance. International communism, controlled and directed from Moscow, represented 'a massive, ideologically based assault upon everything Americans valued.' Business, political, even religious institutions, along with family ties and private ownership were all at stake in this struggle. 'We, as citizens of the world, are engaged today in the most colossal struggle for the control of men's thinking that the world has ever seen,' journalist Saville Davis warned readers of the *Harvard Business Review*.
>
> (Spector 2008: 319)

The threat the Soviet Union represented to the concept of social good based on self-interest within capitalist ideology became pronounced in the Cold War era. There was a need to redefine 'social good' in a way that went beyond self-interest. The need for big business, which was the backbone of advanced capitalist societies such as the USA, to transcend the boundaries of profit maximization and contribute to society outside the market place was not felt so intensely before the Cold War era. The need for big business to contribute to society also became urgent due to the great economic depression of the 1930s, which prompted distrust of the free market economy within advanced capitalist societies. This was the time when socialism was gaining ground within the developing as well as the developed world.

In the context of the Cold War and ideological contestation over the concept of 'social good' and mechanisms to achieve it, business leaders proclaimed their responsibility for both their business and the world. By fulfilling social responsibilities, corporations could fight the spread of totalitarian communism (Spector 2008). Spector argues that:

> Cold War ideology viewed communism as a clear and present danger that threatened world good. By supporting and encouraging free-market values, by fighting the spread of seditious and anti-capitalist points of view, and by opening trade and development with underserved regions in the global marketplace, business leaders could proclaim themselves to be

agents of worldwide benefit in a way that also served their more immediate interests.

(Spector 2008: 319)

Furthermore, it is no coincidence that the capitalist world up to World War II did not have a comprehensive theory regarding the issues faced by the poor (Malik 2011). The capitalist theory regarding the poor (especially those in developing countries) that emerged after World War II was also a Cold War construct. Though 'a number of Western economists had been interested in the economy and social structure of the colonies, and this is hardly surprising given the long history of colonialism' (Baber 2001: 3), comprehensive theories for studying how developing countries could be transformed into developed ones had yet to emerge within Western social science (Malik 2011).

In the USA, knowledge of developing countries barely existed at that time (Wiarda 1999 as cited in Malik 2011). This was because (as mentioned in the introductory chapter) the importance of the developing world in terms of its development along modern lines was recognized only in the mid-twentieth century and 'up until this period there was an almost total absence of systematic theories which attempted to understand and explain the process and trajectory of change from 'developing' to 'developed' societies' (Baber 2001: 3).

It is generally agreed that the emergence of development studies was an outcome of the Cold War global political situation (Wiarda 1999, Baber 2001, as cited in Malik 2011). In the context of the Soviet Revolution and the revolution in the making in China, devising models and theories of development as alternatives to those offered by Marxism – particularly in the light of the popularity Marxism was gaining in the Third World – became imperative for the USA (Wiarda 1999, as cited in Malik 2011).[1] While the focus of Marxist theory was the poor, Western capitalist countries did not have any comparable theory to offer. This was the time when Marxism was gaining ground in the newly independent nations of the Third World. Commenting on the global political situation at that time, Wiarda (1999: 5, as cited in Malik 2011) states:

> During the early years of the Cold War American foreign policy had largely focused on the possibility of a direct confrontation with the Soviet Union; hence Europe and the North Atlantic Treaty Organization (NATO) had received most of the attention. But during the late 1950s and early 1960s, with such important countries in mind as Egypt, Iran, Indonesia, the Philippines, the Congo (later, Zaire), and Cuba (then experiencing the revolution of Fidel Castro), US policy began to realize the main locus of Cold War conflict was likely to be the Third World with its guerrilla revolutions, Marxist nationalism, and anti-imperialism – often in proxy wars using local forces as stand-ins for the United States and the Soviet Union. Moreover, the US government quickly realized that it had little in the way of an attractive model to offer the developing nations as an alternative to Marxism.

Development as a political goal, therefore, came into being in the mid-twentieth century (Mogens & Lauridsen 2012). Mogens & Lauridsen (2012) have argued that there are two significant periods (1950s–1970s and 1980s–2000s) of development and the study of development. The first period from the 1950s to the 1970s was characterized by 'national developmentalism'. The modernization paradigm was the mainstream development model that social scientists such as Parsons and Rostow later promoted in the 1950s and 1960s. In short, the science of 'developmentalism' was created to offer what Rostow's book's title identifies as *The State of Economic Growth: a Non-Communist Manifesto* (Malik 2011).

The overall emphasis of modernization was economic growth and industrialization. The model was based on an assumption that by imitating modern Western process of development, 'less developed nations would gradually transform the traditional societies into the qualities of the modern advanced nations' (Mogens & Lauridsen 2012: 293). The state was seen as the engine of economic growth and industrialization.

The modernization project was criticized by dependency and post-development theorists. They argued that modernization theorists blamed the internal socio-cultural and socio-economic factors in developing societies for underdevelopment, without taking into account external factors such the lengthy period of exploitative colonial rule in these countries. Dependency theorists focused on external economic and political relationships to explain underdevelopment, i.e. underdevelopment was an outcome of the relationship between former colonies and metropolitan powers. They argued that development based on the modernisation project was actually a process of 'underdevelopment' or 'dependent development' determined by the dominant industrial countries in the North.

For post-development thinkers, development cannot be understood as an objective phenomenon independent of the academic discourse that theorizes it. The exercise of power is implicit in the ways that development is theorized and how the categories and representations created are naturalized through discourse. They accuse the discourse of development of increasing poverty and inequality, creating vast urban-rural differences, environmental degradation, rampant consumerism of the elite and cultural conflict. Post-development scholars such as Escobar (1995), therefore, argue for an alternative to development instead of alternative development.

In the second period, 1980s–2000s, the development project according to Hansen and Lauridsen 'was replaced by the globalization project that prioritized free markets, private property and individual incentives' (Mogens & Lauridsen 2012: 294). International governance was characterized by the neoliberal economic order. Though there was vast disparity between developed and developing countries in terms of economic development, both 'were supposed to play by the same set of rules and mainstream development theory was opposed to developing a separate body of economics for developing countries' … . [The] state was still important but now as the main obstacle to development' (Mogens & Lauridsen 2012: 294).

Following Sen's (1999) capability approach, others endeavored to bring equity, poverty and employment back to the forefront by developing sustainable human development-centered theory. Other approaches such as 'alternative development', which criticized developmentalism in both its neoliberal and pre-neoliberal forms, were also advanced. Alternative development suggested society should serve human beings and nature rather than the market.

Overall, in the nearly three decades since the end of the Cold War, the world has witnessed a remarkable rejection of the big plans and projects that characterized the period of high-modernization that existed between the Bretton Woods pact of 1944 and the end of the par value system in 1971. In place of hydroelectric engineering feats, geographically based industrial zones and political experiments in 'Third World welfare states', a multitude of social policy initiatives and international development programmes based on the neoliberal economic paradigm tied to smaller, more efficient, face-to-face, culturally appropriate and voluntary civil society-based organizations have proliferated. This has spawned a mass of buzzwords, acronyms and theoretical assumptions such as social capital, capacity building, governance and accountability, empowerment, participatory development, and non-governmental, community-based, and third sector organizations (NGOs, CBOs). These new civil society approaches to international development assistance have become ubiquitous across all sectors of the development industry, from small grassroots organizations to large multilateral donors such as the World Bank and the International Monetary Fund.

This civil society approach to international development assistance is part of the good governance paradigm that advocates a lean state and a greater role for the market. In this connection, therefore, the role of CSR in development has become central for business organizations, development agencies, the United Nations and international financial institutions.

Though the concept of CSR has been under discussion since the 1950s, it came under the spotlight due to the Cold War situation and the social activism of the 1960s and 1970s. People seemed to be hopeful that business would eventually have a responsibility to them outside their economic role in the market place (Manne 1972, as cited in Ali *et al.* 2010: 477). Drucker (1974) argues that corporations started to respond to the view that they had a responsibility to pay something back to the public. The concept of corporate social responsibility generally requires the business community to follow moral principles to minimize problems in the business environment and maximize the public good (Rondinelli & Berry 2000). Rondinelli & Berry argued that corporate operations could affect the environment negatively, so corporations need to act responsibly to protect the environment. Esty & Winston (2009) have demonstrated how environmentally conscious 'smart' companies use environmental strategy to innovate, create value, and build competitive advantage. Beurden & Gössling (2008) on the other hand conducted a literature survey of the link between CSR and companies' financial performance. Their survey revealed empirical evidence for a positive correlation between

CSR and financial performance. They argued, therefore, that for Western societies, good ethics is good business.

In the 1980s, fewer new definitions of CSR emerged and the emphasis was more on measuring and conducting research on CSR (Carroll 1999). In the 1990s, 'the CSR concept transitioned significantly to alternative themes such as stakeholder theory, business ethics theory, and corporate citizenship' (Carroll 1999: 292). Carroll notes that during this period writers did not reject the CSR concept, but there were no new definitions added to the body of literature.

Overall, however, despite ongoing efforts to define CSR, it still defies clear-cut definition. Dahlsrud (2008) developed an index of 37 definitions of CSR and argued that none of the definitions define the social responsibility of business but 'rather describe CSR as a phenomenon' (Dahlsrud 2008: 6). He concludes that 'this might be the cause of the definitional confusion: it is not so much a confusion of how CSR is defined, as it is about what constitutes the social responsibility of business' (Dahlsrud 2008: 6). Pointing to CSR as an elusive concept, Kitchin (2002, as cited in Wan-Jan 2006: 176–7) states:

> One moment (CSR) seems to mean the engagement of nongovernmental organizations (NGOs), the next it is all about charitable donations, and five minutes later, it seems to mean the ethical treatment of employees. One minute the NGOs are calling the shots, the next the accountants are in on the act selling reputation assurance

Broadly defined, CSR is about fulfilling business social obligations towards society. However, there is much less certainty about what these obligations or their scope might be (Smith 2003: 3). This uncertainty emerges out of a mix of business motivations which Smith (2003) differentiates as 'business case' and 'normative case'. Similarly, Wan-Jan (2006) divides literature on CSR into two categories depending on the way CSR is perceived: 1) CSR as an ethical position, and 2) CSR as a business strategy. In Smith's terminology, the ethical position would refer to a 'normative case' and 'business strategy' to a 'business case'. Wan-Jan identifies scholars such as Mintzberg (1983, 2002) and Moore (2003) who present CSR as an ethical stance and Friedman (1970), Henderson (2001, 2004) and Lantos (2001, 2003) who present CSR as business strategy.

Wan-Jan reports that according to Mintzberg (1983), CSR could appear in four forms. The purest form is when firms practise CSR without any expectation of reward, because 'that is the noble way for corporations to behave' (Mintzberg 1983, as cited in Wan-Jan 2006: 178). The second form is characterized by 'enlightened self-interest'. In this form, firms expect that there would be payback for firms from CSR. The 'pay could be tangible or intangible but in either case, the payback is expected' (Wan-Jan 2006: 178). According to Wan-Jan (2006: 178), this refers to Mintzberg's third form of CSR, 'in which CSR is seen as a sound investment'. The stock market reacts to firms' decisions regarding 'sound investment' according to 'sound investment theory' and firms pursuing CSR are rewarded by the market (Wan-Jan 2006: 178). The fourth form, related to 'enlightened self-interest', is to practice CSR 'in order to avoid interference from external political influences' and 'prevent authorities forcing them to [do] so via legislation' (Wan-Jan 2006: 178).

As stated by Wan-Jan, Mintzberg accepts CSR in its purest form and rejects other forms of CSR as being unethical. He argues that CSR should only be practised from an ethical stance, without expectation of returns. To Mintzberg, 'CSR means firms undertaking some actions to service society beyond selfishness and greed' (Wan-Jan 2006: 178).

Moore (2003) went a step further by arguing that CSR for profitability would mean 'putting virtue at the service of avarice' (as cited in Wan-Jan 2006: 178). He argued that, by pursuing CSR, firms are actually trying to ease the tension that exists between society and firms' economic endeavours (Wan-Jan 2006: 178).

Apart from Mintzberg and Moore, Wan-Jan (2006) mentions Goyder (2003), who articulated his concerns by establishing two categories of CSR: 'compliance CSR' and 'conviction CSR'. The basic motivation for firms behind 'compliance CSR' is image-building to assure their stakeholders that they are conscious of societal needs. The actual aim, however, is instrumental, i.e. that if they invest in CSR activities they need to be rewarded. Contrarily, following 'conviction CSR', firms would do something for society without any expectation of payback. Firms 'that subscribe to 'conviction CSR' will ensure that they have positive impacts on 'people, the natural world, and the planet' (Goyder 2003: 4, as cited in Wan-Jan 2006: 178).

Overall, CSR today is not considered mere corporate philanthropy and CSR is no longer peripheral to companies' operations in the industrially developed world. Legal compliance requirements are increasing. Increasing the number of stakeholders in a firm is leading to increased accountability of firms to their stakeholders.

Riordan & Fairbrass (2008: 745), with reference to increasing pressures from media, governments and non-governmental organisations (NGOs), suggest that 'Part of the burden of addressing the demands of CSR is the need to engage effectively with a range of stakeholders'. Developing effective CSR stakeholder dialogue strategies and practices has become an important task for companies; for some, such as those within the pharmaceutical and oil industries, it has become ever more important and complex.

To address the increasing complexity of stakeholders expectations, enterprises are encouraged to adopt a long-term, strategic approach to CSR and to explore the opportunities for developing innovative products, services and business models that contribute to societal well-being. In essence, the CSR movement, at least in the advanced industrial countries of the North, refers to how companies manage their business processes to produce an overall positive impact – whether in the form of economic growth and distribution or as community development, capacity-building or environmental or human rights protection – on society. However, how societies in developing countries define the 'overall positive impact' of CSR and prioritize different aspects of their social responsibility is still uncertain.

In light of the above, it becomes important to ask whether CSR, which is primarily a Western construct, is practised in the same way in developing economies. Indeed, 'we should be careful not to superimpose Western notions of CSR on the reality in emerging economies' (Frynas 2006: 17). Philanthropy is a key example. In Europe, the notion of philanthropy is not regarded as part of core CSR activities, whereas companies in emerging economies are expected to actively assist their local communities (Frynas 2006: 17). More-over, 'the motives for CSR and actual CSR practice may have a peculiar local flavour in emerging economies' (Frynas 2006: 17). For example, companies in Malaysian are at least partly motivated by ideas of business practice advo-cated in Islamic religion and in the case of Pakistan this reality is even more prominent. Frynas (2006: 18), therefore, suggests that:

> We may need to develop new ways of assessing the social contribution of business in societies other than our own in order to capture corporate activities that do not conveniently fall under the umbrella of FTSF4Good or GRI (Global Reporting Initiative) criteria. Otherwise, we run the risk of weakening long-established and intrinsic social obligations, which could perhaps provide a more lasting impact on corporate behavior than externally imposed codes of practice.

Conclusions

The origin of modern corporate social responsibility is in the industrially advanced countries of the North. The concept has been under discussion since the 1950s, coming under the spotlight due to the Cold War situation and the social activism of the 1960s and 1970s. This was because the Soviet Union posed a real threat to the concept of 'social good' based on self-interest within capitalist ideology in the Cold War era. The need to redefine 'social good' beyond self-interest – for big business, especially in the USA, to transcend the boundaries of profit maximization and contribute to society outside the market – was important. This need also became urgent due to the great eco-nomic depression of the 1930s, which caused advanced capitalist societies to mistrust the free market economy. This is the time when socialism was gaining ground within the developing and the developed world.

In the 1980s, fewer new definitions of CSR emerged and the emphasis was more on measuring and conducting research on CSR (Carroll 1999). In the 1990s, alternative themes such as stakeholder theory, business ethics theory and 'corporate citizenship' were added to the list of definitions in the body of literature on CSR

Similarly, ideas related to developing countries' development emerged in the mid-twentieth century in the context of the Cold War and the threat from the Soviet Union. Marxism offered a comprehensive theory of the development of the poor, but capitalism lacked any such theory. The need for an alternative theory of development in this area became urgent and 'development studies' as a new field of inquiry into the problems of the poor in developing countries was introduced in the USA to compete with Soviet Marxism. The paradigm of development evolved from modernization initiated by the state in developing countries to a multitude of social policy initiatives and development programmes based on the neoliberal economic paradigm tied to smaller, more efficient, face-to-face, culturally appropriate and voluntary civil society-based organizations have proliferated. Such a transition was the result of a good-governance paradigm that advocated a lean state and a greater role for the market.

As part of this, the role of CSR in development has become central the world over. However, it would be wrong to expect that CSR, being primarily a Western construct, can be practiced in the same way in developing economies. Following Frynas (2006), we need to be careful not to superimpose Western notions of CSR on the reality in developing countries such as Pakistan. Learning from the experiences of advanced industrial countries, it needs to be developed organically from within the society.

Note

1 Needless to say, the Soviet experiment in human development also failed in the long run. The above statement, therefore, simply describes the challenge the USA encountered in relation to the development of the poor vis-à-vis the Soviet interpretation of Marxism and its growing popularity in developing countries.

3   The state of development in Pakistan

This chapter provides a rationale for enhanced CSR activities through information and analysis of underdevelopment in Pakistan. Pakistan is in a period of conspicuous political, economic and socio-religious conflict. The country faces multiple imbalances, with critical issues being an uncontrollable law and order situation, the militarization of state and society, drug trafficking, ethnic-sectarian violence, religious extremism, terrorism and violence against women and minorities. Terrorism in Pakistan has significantly diverted resources from development to security.

According to the Human Rights Commission of Pakistan (HRCP 2013), ethnic, sectarian, terrorist and politically linked violence killed or wounded more than 8,000 people in 2012. More than 6,400 people were killed or injured in 2013 in sectarian and terrorist violence alone (Behn 2013). Moreover, there were between 240 and 400 casualties from 48 American drone attacks in tribal areas on the border with Afghanistan in 2012 (Behn 2013).

Pakistan's economy is grappling with continual dilapidation due to structural problems, a domestic energy crisis, decline in investment, persistent high inflation (ten per cent in 2012) and security issues. The budget deficit and losses by state-owned enterprises remain high compared to tax revenue (Daily Times 2012). Pakistan Railways, Pakistan International Airlines and Pakistan Steel Mills have incurred steep losses for the past several years. The challenge of improving efficiency and putting these enterprises on a viable commercial footing is formidable. Due to electricity and gas shortages and security issues, gross fixed investment has declined for four years, from about 21 per cent of gross domestic product (GDP) in the financial year 2007 to 12 per cent of GDP in FY2012 (Daily Times 2012).

Pakistan was born at a time of chaos. Hundreds of thousands of migrant Hindus, Sikhs and Muslims, both in India and Pakistan, were killed as a consequence of the largest human migration of modern times. In view of this, it seems that a country birthed in chaos has now been overtaken by it, 66 years later.

Poverty and inequality in Pakistan

Poverty in Pakistan is at a historic high. Every third Pakistani is in the 'poor' bracket, with some 58.7 million out of a total population of 180 million subsisting below the poverty line (Dawn 2012). This includes more than half the population in remote Balochistan, 33 per cent in Sindh and 32 per cent in Khyber Pakhtunkhwa (Dawn 2012). Besides the increase in overall poverty, what is important to note is the lack of meaningful, non-discriminatory representation of all provinces in decision-making, adding to the drivers of poverty. Inequitable resource distribution to provinces has been a major cause of ethnic conflict and has strengthened terrorist groups in Pakistan (Rashid 2009: 1). The port city of Karachi, with a population of 17 million people, 'is an ethnic and sectarian tinderbox waiting to explode' (Rashid 2009: 1). The city is almost entirely controlled by hundreds of criminal, mafia and religious extremist groups. The worst sufferers are the poor.

There are several measures by which we can judge the state of income inequality in the economy. Economists usually use one principal measure of income distribution, which is called size distribution. Size distribution of income means the total income of individuals and households.

Inequality in distribution of income over the years is given in Table 3.1. To understand the data in Table 3.1 and how it indicates inequality it is important to understand the concept of the 'Gini coefficient'. Economists calculate size distribution of income by the Gini coefficient. The Gini coefficient is an aggregate inequality measure and can vary by anything from zero to one. When the Gini coefficient is 'zero', it means that there is absolute equality,

Table 3.1 Income inequality

Year	Household Gini coefficient
1963/4	0.386
1966/7	0.355
1968/9	0.336
1969/70	0.336
1970/1	0.33
1971/2	0.345
1979	0.373
1984/5	0.369
1985/6	0.355
1986/7	0.346
1987/8	0.348
1990/1	0.407
1992/3	0.41
1993/4	0.4
1996/7	0.4
1998/9	0.41
2000/1	0.28
2004/5	0.3
2005/6	0.3

Source: Economic Survey of Pakistan 2000–01 and 2007–08, Pakistan Bureau of Statistics, Government of Pakistan

and when it is 'one', it means that there is absolute inequality. In order words, we can say that an increase in the Gini coefficient indicates an increase in inequality. The inequality data for after the 2005/6 period are not available.

Table 3.1 indicates the extent of inequality in income distribution over the years. It clearly illustrates that the highest inequality in Pakistan was during the decade of the 1990s, when the Gini coefficient rose to 0.4 or above. In the previous decades, the trend in inequality had been fluctuating. This means that in some years it went up and in others it went down. For example during the 1960s, the highest inequality was during 1963/4 when the Gini coefficient was 0.386. This went down in the later years and then again rose to 0.373 in 1979. Overall, however, inequality remained low in the 1970s compared to the 1960s. The decade of the 1980s again saw a decrease in inequality because of improvements in income distribution, mainly due to large gains from foreign aid during the Afghan war. Overall, however, inequality was greater during the 1980s than the 1970s. From the 1990s onwards inequality in income distribution significantly increased and the Gini coefficient remained above 0.4. It declined in 2000/1 and again rose to 0.30 in 2005/6.

The varying trends in inequality from the 1960s to the 1990s were mainly due to a haphazard pattern of economic growth and political instability. During the 1990s, apart from political and economic instability, the other factor worsening the inequitable distribution of income was unequal distribution of income between professionals (white-collar workers) and non-professionals. According to official statistics, there was strong growth in the category of highly skilled professionals across all non-agricultural sectors, particularly in multinationals and the social services sector.

Moreover, evidence shows that the IMF Structural Adjustment Programme (SAP) also increased poverty. SAP introduced the policy paradigm of stabilization and import liberalization, which significantly increased indirect taxes and the cost of production of locally manufactured goods, causing a decline in local manufacturing and leading to a decline in employment and real wage rates. All these factors contributed significantly to an increase in poverty.

Though the inequality data is not available after 2005–06, we can use data available, calculated through another method, in which we see the range of consumption by the bottom 20 percent and top 20 percent of the population. This ratio is often used as a measure of inequality between the two extremes of very poor and very rich in the country. According to Pakistan Federal Bureau of Statistics, Household Integrated Economic Survey 2011–12 (HIES), among total households, those with highest income level have more than three times income on averaged as compared to lowest income households in urban and rural areas (see PBS 2011–12: 7). The disaggregated data on per capita consumption expenditure in urban and rural areas provided by the same source reveals that the average individual expenditures for the richest quintile in urban areas are four and a half times more than the poorest quintile. Similarly, for rural areas it is more than three and a half times the poorest quintile. There 'is not much difference between the average per capita expenditure for the poorest quintile in rural and urban areas, whereas it is higher in urban areas than the rural areas for the richest quintile' (see PBS 2011–12:8).

Share of income and employment

The current employment situation represents an enormous waste of resources and an unacceptable level of human suffering. It has led to growing social exclusion, rising inequality and a host of social evils (United Nations Development Programme, *Human Development Report*, 2011)

Poverty and unemployment are considered twins. In Pakistan, unemployment as well as underemployment has risen to a critical state. A major part of the labour force is unemployed or underemployed. Unemployed persons do not contribute their share in national income and create social and political unrest in the country. Unemployed persons, besides losing income, suffer from boredom, depression, family tension, divorce and violence and have a tendency to criminality.

Pakistan has the ninth largest labour force in the world (ESoP 2013). The labour force survey for 2012 was not published; the total labour force in the country was 57.24 million according to the 2010–11 labour force survey (ESoP 2013). In 2011 there were 3.40 million unemployed people and 53.84 million were employed, out of the total labour force (ESoP 2013): for details see Table 3.2. However, the unemployment rate decreased marginally from 7.7 per cent in 2003/4 to 5.9 per cent in 2010/11 (ESoP 2013).

Major causes:

- The population of Pakistan is rising on the fast track. About one million new people are entering the job market each year. Meanwhile, expansion in employment opportunities is not enough to absorb all the new job seekers, so the unemployment rate is on the rise.
- The investment rate is also declining, and since the rate of increase in investment and income produces a multiplier effect on the economy, the decline in investment is giving rise to poverty and unemployment.
- In Pakistan, the majority of people are uneducated and have no skills relevant to a particular job. Most of the students opt for general education and wish to get white-collar jobs in an office. They are not interested in vocational training. When they leave education they have degrees but no work, training or employment opportunities. Since the level of literacy and enrolments are low and the government's poverty reduction policies have proved to be inadequate, a poor person has few chances of finding employment or creating self-employment.

Table 3.2 Civilian labour force, employed and unemployed, for Pakistan (in millions)

	2003/4	2005/6	2006/7	2007/8	2008/9	2009/10	2010/11
Labour force	45.5	50.05	50.33	51.78	53.72	56.33	57.24
Employed	42	46.95	47.65	49.09	50.79	53.21	53.84
Unemployed	3.5	3.1	2.68	2.69	2.93	3.12	3.4

Source: Labour force surveys as cited in Chapter 12, 'Population, Labour Force and Employment', in ESoP 2013

Rural poverty

The most valid generalization about the poor is that they are disproportionately located in rural areas and primarily engaged in agricultural and associated activities; women and children are poorer than adult males. Findings show that about three-quarters of the very poor scratch out their livelihood from subsistence agriculture, as either small farmers or low-paid farm workers. Some of the remaining one-third are also located in rural areas but engaged in petty services, and others are located on the fringes and in marginal areas of urban centres, where they engage in various forms of self-employment such as street-hawking, trading, petty services and small-scale commerce.

Nearly half the population live on less than one US dollar a day. Socio-economic indicators are substantially worse for women and children. Around 67.5 per cent of the population in Pakistan depends directly on agriculture. Of the total number of farmers, roughly 93 per cent own just 36 per cent of the land and live on the minimum level of income. Ever since independence, due to the inept policies of various governments, there has been no real effort to improve agriculture and the farming community is suffering. The result is low productivity and low returns to farmers, pushing a vast majority of them to live below the poverty line. Moreover, due to this situation, villagers are moving into urban areas, which increases the complexity of problems there.

Several generalizations can be made about the incidence of poverty in rural Pakistan:

1. The rural landless, share-cropping tenants and wage workers represent a majority of those who can be regarded as functionally vulnerable, and a high proportion of them are living in poverty.
2. While not all the rural landless are without assets, such as livestock-husbandry or other skills, those who depend on manual labour may be experiencing particularly severe poverty. Agricultural labourers and low-skilled manual workers are perhaps the most vulnerable groups in rural society.
3. Small resource-poor farmers account for perhaps one third of the functionally vulnerable in the rural population. Their dependence on wage labour has become an important source of household income.

4. Among the owners and operators of land, including tenants, some 75–80 per cent of household income is generated in agriculture. But, considering the total population, more than one half of low-income households now come from non-agricultural sources as well.

Women's development

Of a total population of 183 million in 2012, women comprised almost half: 48.7 per cent. It is therefore impossible to visualize any meaningful development or progress at national level without their optimum participation, but unfortunately reality is very far from such a state of affairs.

The total labour force in Pakistan in 2012 was 58 million (HRCP 2012). This number grows by around 3 per cent every year. Wage employees represented 37.1 per cent of the workforce, the self-employed 23.1 per cent and farmers 39.8 per cent (HRCP 2012). The unemployment rate in Pakistan decreased to 6 per cent in the second quarter of 2013 from 6.30 per cent in the first quarter of 2013 (PBS 2013). From 1985 to 2013 the unemployment rate averaged 5.4 per cent, reaching an all-time high of 7.8 per cent in June 2002 and a record low of 3.1 per cent in December 1987. In Pakistan, the unemployment rate measures the number of people actively looking for a job as a percentage of the labour force.

The largest number of unemployed persons are women who suffer due to both lack of employment opportunities and cultural barriers. Out of the total number of women of working age in Pakistan only 28 per cent are active workers; the majority of these are employed as domestic help (HRCP 2012). This significantly adds to women's poverty.

Another indicator of the disparity between men and women is the difference in their literacy rates. According to the Human Rights Commission of Pakistan's 2012 annual report (HRCP 2012), the literacy rate for girls was 42 per cent and for boys 74 per cent. Furthermore:

> In Khyber Pakhtunkhwa, at least 20 girls' schools were shut down in 2012 in remote locations of Charsadda district due to a shortage of teachers. In a concrete step for girls' schooling, the Khyber Pakhtunkhwa government allocated 70% of its education budget for female education, which was expected to help rebuild all the girls' schools that had been destroyed by militants in the province. In Balochistan, where the dropout rate for children in schools was very high, only 23% girls were enrolled in primary schools. Due to a scarcity of girls' middle and high schools along with problems of transport, many girls were forced to abandon their education.
>
> (HRCP 2012: 168)

As well as fewer opportunities for employment and education, women are not able to fulfill their social and psychological needs. They have no healthy life or social identity. In addition, women are not secure – poor women's financial resources are meagre and unstable relative to men's.

The poorest segments of Pakistan's population live in households headed by women, in which there are generally no male wage earners. The proportion is rising throughout most of Pakistan. Because the earning potential of women is considerably below that of their male counterparts, women are more likely to be among the very poor. In general, large households have less education, lower incomes and higher fertility. In the case of divorce, there is a greater strain on the woman as single parent.

A portion of income disparity between male- and female-headed households can be explained by the large earning differentials between men and women, in addition to the fact that women are often paid less for performing similar tasks. They are essentially barred from higher-paying occupations. Similarly, rural women have less access to the resources necessary to generate stable incomes and are frequently subject to laws that further compromise earning potential. With a few notable exceptions, government employment or income-enhancing programmes are only accessible to men, increasing existing income disparities between men and women.

The degree of economic hardship may also vary widely within a household. It is important to note that household income is a poor measure of individual welfare because the distribution of income within the household may be quite unequal. In fact, among the poor, the economic status of women is a better indicator of their welfare, as well as that of their children. For example, in many regions of Pakistan there exists a strong bias against females in areas such as nutrition, medical treatment, education and inheritance. Moreover, the gender biases in household resource allocation significantly reduce the rate of survival among female infants. Women's control over household income and resources is limited for a number of reasons. Of primary importance is the fact that a relatively large proportion of the work performed by women is unremunerated.

It is common for the male head of the household to control all funds from cash crops or the family business, even if his spouse provides a significant portion of the labour input. In addition, in many areas in Pakistan, it is considered socially unacceptable for women to contribute significantly to household income, and hence women's work remains concealed or unrecognized. These combined factors perpetuate the low economic status of women and can lead to strict limitations on their control over household resources.

In urban areas too, training programmes to increase earning potential and formal sector employment are generally limited to men, while agricultural extension programmes promote male-dominated crops, frequently at the expense of women's vegetable plots. Consequently, women and their dependents remain the most economically vulnerable group in the country.

Prevalent development policy underscores the importance of integrating women into development programmes at all levels. To improve living conditions for the poorest individuals, women's participation in educational training programmes, formal sector employment, and agriculture and extension programme needs to be increased. It is also of primary importance that precautions are taken to ensure that women have equal access to government resources provided through schooling, services, employment and security programmes. Moreover, all discriminatory laws against women need to be abolished, as they are obstacles to women's social and economic participation in the nation-building process.

Decline in women's relative or absolute economic status has both ethical and long-term economic implications. Any process of growth that fails to improve the welfare of the people experiencing the greatest hardships, broadly recognized to be women and children, fails to accomplish one of the principal goals of development. In the long run, the low status of women is likely to translate into slower rates of economic growth. The benefits of current investments in human capital are more likely to be passed on to future generations if women are successfully integrated into the growth process. And considering that human capital is perhaps the most important prerequisite for growth, education and enhanced economic status for women are critical to meeting long-term development objectives.

Social indicators (health, education and housing)

Health

Social development has been one of the major policy objectives of different governments and administrations in Pakistan. The fact that social development in Pakistan has lagged behind remains a grim reality, though, and the health sector is no exception. The trajectory of its budgetary allocation has been progressively downwards. Statistics from the Economic Survey of Pakistan 2012–13 indicate a decline in the percentage of GDP being allocated to health from 0.72 per cent in the fiscal year 2000/1 to 0.35 per cent in the fiscal year 2012/13. The current ratio of population density versus health facilities is at 1127 persons per one doctor, 14406 per dentist and the availability of one hospital bed for 1786 persons (ESoP 2013: 147).

The infant mortality rate in Pakistan is high compared to several other developing countries. Table 3.3 indicates gaps in well-being and life chances in Pakistan in comparison with other countries in the region. Health outcomes in Pakistan are poor compared to other countries listed. A higher population growth of 2.0 per cent is one of the factors that account for poorer progress. Life expectancy in Pakistan was 65.5 years in 2012. Indicators relating to child mortality and maternal health show poor progress as well (ESoP 2013).

A key aspect is the fact that the impact of this failure in the health sector has been unequally distributed. Given that the poor lack the capacity to access the market for their needs and basic services, the success or failure of state-level social policies, plans and schemes has a direct impact on their welfare.

Table 3.3 Regional countries human development indicators

Country	Life Expectancy 2012	Infant Mortality Rate Per 1000 2011	Under 5 Mortality Rate Per 1000 2011	Maternal Mortality Rate Per 100000 2010	Population Growth Rate (%) 2012
Pakistan	65.7	59	72	260	2.03*
India	65.8	47	61	200	1.31
Bangladesh	69.2	37	46	240	1.58
Sri Lanka	75.1	11	12	35	0.91
Nepal	69.1	39	48	170	1.77
Bhutan	68	42	54	180	1.18
China	73.7	13	15	37	0.48
Malaysia	74.5	6	7	29	1.57
Indonesia	69.8	25	32	220	1.03
Philippines	69	20	25	99	1.87
Thailand	74.3	11	12	48	0.54

Source: Human Development Report 2013 & UNICEF
* National Institute of Population (NIP)

The history of social development in the country is beset with policies, plans, programmes, projects and schemes. The main emphasis of development plans has been to increase the quantity rather than the quality of health-related services, such as the number of doctors, rural health centres and basic health units.

Another reason why people living in absolute poverty, especially in the rural areas, are deprived of basic health facilities is because of the fiscal constraints evident at all tiers of government. Thanks to the Structural Adjustment Programme's stabilization changes to the economy, continued under Pakistan's 'good governance' initiatives, expenditure on the social sector was greatly reduced, leading to poor social sector development. The negative effects of all the above-related problems, accumulated overtime, can be observed through Pakistan's media. Daily newspapers are filled with reports such as a boy killed because of malaria, a woman wrongly operated on by quacks or dehydration and heatstroke causing the death of an infant; these sorry stories usually come out of the rural areas of Pakistan.

Lipton calls this phenomenon 'urban bias' (see Lipton 1977). This exists not only in health but also in other social sector policies adopted by the government. The phenomenon is prevalent for several reasons. The major reason is that the ruling class – members of the government, the bureaucracy and the military – have made urban areas their power base and the infrastructure has been developed to support them, while people with meagre incomes, who sometimes survive on less than a dollar a day, are usually inhabitants of rural areas. These helpless people, because they cannot afford food or shelter, do not effectively voice their demand for increasing and improving health facilities in their areas because this option is very low on their priority list.

Urban bias is further strengthened by the other determinant, which is 'class bias'. This is the reason that not all urban people have equal access to good health care. There are slum dwellers in cities who live in conditions similar to those in village communities. Slum dwellers may be better off in the sense that they are aware of the health facilities provided, but worse off because most of those facilities are beyond their means. Hence, even for residents within cities there are great differences in access to services.

The problem does not end there. The ruling class in urban areas essentially determines the dynamics of the health sector. Consequently, water-borne diseases such as cholera, typhoid and malaria and easily cured illnesses such as stomach infections and heatstroke, pervasive in rural areas, are neglected. Simple diarrhea kills one out of every 12 children born into poor and uneducated households before they are five years old. Similarly, so-called 'eradicated' diseases like TB remain fatal in Pakistan.

Given the need to promote social development and health care, the government must continue to own its large asset base in the health sector, and this the government cannot do without the assistance of the private sector to provide facilities to the masses – not only in cities but also in rural areas.

Although the government has on its own introduced several programmes it still has a long way to go. In addition, since the profit motive drives much of the health industry, some sort of taxation or cross-subsidization will have to be introduced to support the efforts of the government in providing health care to those who cannot afford the higher private-sector prices. Hence, the public-private partnership philosophy has the potential to be very productive in the health sector, and the corporate sector can play a significant role in this direction.

Education

Another social sector that is a cornerstone of broad-base economic growth and poverty reduction is education. No nation can take advantage of trade and development opportunities in a rapidly integrating economy without major advances in education. At the same time, without rapid and substantial improvement in access to education, the quality of broader poverty reduction efforts will be blunted.

To meet the Millennium Development Goal regarding education, the Pakistan National Education Policy 2009 aimed to bring the literacy rate up to 86 per cent by 2015. It further stated that Pakistan would achieve universal primary education by ensuring zero drop-out rates at primary level (ESoP 2013). According to the latest Pakistan Social and Living Standards Measurement (PSLM) Survey 2011–12 (as cited in ESoP 2013), however, the literacy rate of the population (ten years old and above) remained at 58 per cent in 2011–12. As Table 3.4 indicates, it seems that the literacy MDGs will not be achievable by 2015. Moreover, during this period, literacy remained

Table 3.4 Literacy rate (ten-year-olds and older), Pakistan and provinces (in percentages)

Province/Area	2010/11			2011/12		
	Male	Female	Total	Male	Female	Total
Pakistan	69	46	58	70	47	58
Rural	63	35	49	64	35	49
Urban	81	67	74	82	68	75
Punjab	70	51	60	70	51	60
Rural	64	42	53	65	41	52
Urban	80	71	76	80	70	75
Sindh	71	46	59	72	47	60
Rural	60	22	42	58	23	41
Urban	82	68	75	85	70	78
KPK	68	33	50	72	35	52
Rural	67	29	48	70	31	50
Urban	77	50	63	80	51	65
Balochistan	60	19	41	65	23	46
Rural	54	13	35	60	16	40
Urban	79	40	61	79	44	62

Source: Pakistan Social and Living Standards Measurement Survey 2012–13, Pakistan Bureau of Statistics, Government of Pakistan

much higher in urban than in rural areas and much higher for men than women. Province-wide data indicates that the literacy rate is 60 per cent in Punjab and Sindh, 52 per cent in Khyber Pakhtunkhwa and 46 per cent in Balochistan. In short, the traditional disparity among provinces remains. Overall, in terms of Pakistan's literacy world ranking, it stands 113th among 120 nations.

Regarding net enrolment, the Pakistan National Education Policy 2009 had targeted 100 per cent net primary enrolment of children aged 5–9 years and 100 per cent completion rate of students at primary level. As shown in Table 3.5, this was unachievable and in 2011/12 the enrolment rate remained at 57 per cent. The completion rate for 2011/12 is not available, but the 49 per

Table 3.5 Progress towards MDG 2 at national level (in percentages)

Indicator	2001/02	2004/05	2007/08	2010/11	2011/12	MDG target 2015
Net primary enrolment rate, 5–9 years old	42	52	55	56	57	100
Completion/Survival rate, grade 1 to 5	57.3	67.1	52.3	49	–	100
Literacy rate, 10 years old and above	45	53	56	58	58	88

Source: Pakistan Social and Living Standards Measurement Survey 2011–12, as cited in Chapter 10, 'Education', ESoP 2013

cent completion rate for 2010–11 indicates that the number of students who complete primary education is not yet significant.

Pakistan was spending 2.3 per cent of its GNP and 9.9 per cent of the government budget on education, while India 4.5 was spending per cent of GNP and 12.7 per cent of government budget and Bangladesh 2.1 per cent of GNP and 14.1 per cent of government budget on education (Pakistan Defence 2012). The budget allocated for education for 2013 was Rs 2.6 billion. One of the basic reasons, apart from the meagre budget spent on education generally, has been a lack of emphasis on primary education by successive governments. As a result, the primary school participation rate, according to official statistics, is less than 14 million of the 20 million children belonging to the 5–9 age group enrolled for primary education (HRCP 2013). The actual figure is estimated to be much lower, especially because of drop-out between enrolment and completion. The drop-out rate even according to official figures is as high as 45 per cent at primary level (HRCP 2013). There has been a sharp decline in enrolment, especially at government schools, due to increasing poverty and inadequate standards of education. Enrollment at primary, middle and higher levels were 19.92 million, 4.28 million and 1.7 million respectively (HRCP 2013).

Moreover, there is very evident disparity between enrollment rates in urban and rural areas within the country, creating inequality. This is an outcome of the unequal distribution of resources, higher teacher absenteeism, lack of access and higher opportunity costs for parents in rural areas (where parents have more incentive to send their children to work than to school). Corporal punishment is frequent in government schools, especially in rural areas. As a result, broken limbs and even suicide by students was frequently reported in 2012 (HRCP 2012). Though the Prohibition of Corporal Punishment Act introduced by the government of Pakistan prohibits corporal punishment at schools, the violence continues and is one of the causes of the high drop-out rate in the country.

In addition to the low level of budgetary allocations for education, the difference in enrolment in urban and rural areas and the culture of corporal punishment in government schools, Pakistan's education system is marred by numerous other problems. For example, the textbooks are of a low standard, imparting everything but sound basic knowledge. The curriculum is designed to inculcate communal, ethnic and sectarian hatred in young minds. Moreover, it is gender biased. Such an education system is disempowering rather than empowering people by developing biased and negative views in the minds of young students.

Another problem that lies at the root of the poor education system in Pakistan is the medium of instruction, which is frequently not the child's first language. Young minds experiencing the natural process of learning from their surroundings face a dilemma when an alien language is imposed on them for the rest of their lives. In such a system, where a child does not even have the right to think and learn in his/her own language, s/he miserably fails to develop good communication skills and understanding. This leaves him/her helpless in this rapidly developing and competitive world. Pakistan's policymakers seem oblivious of the damaging effects of such a practice.

The above data indicates that no government, will be able to eradicate the multidimensional problems of poverty in Pakistan unless it educates and empowers its people. However, given the dysfunctional education system and the policies prevalent in the country, the development of human capital seems a far-fetched idea.

The first important step in poverty alleviation is mass literacy through primary education. However, Pakistan's past and present show that nothing much has been done to provide quality primary education. This has got in the way of all attempts to achieve mass literacy and thereby better equip people to participate in nation-building.

Housing

Adequate housing and a healthy environment are basic human needs and the provision of adequate housing is an integral part of any meaningful programme of social and economic development. However, as with the other social sectors discussed above, housing provision in Pakistan is manifestly unequal and once again it is poverty-stricken people who bear the brunt.

The degree of inequality can be gauged from the palatial houses in 'luxury' housing estates at one end of the spectrum and extensive slums at the other end. This inequality in the housing sector is due to several factors.

Since upper-income groups are able to arrange adequate housing for themselves, it is the lower-income groups that are dependent on state provision of plots. This is of some consequence, as over 70 per cent of annual incremental housing demand in urban areas emanates from low-income groups, for whom obtaining developed plots and constructing a house through formal market mechanisms is beyond reach (HRCP 2012). This inequality is partly a product of improper development due to rural-urban migration and partly because of policy failure.

Apart from 'natural' population increase, i.e. the growth in urban families, there is net rural to urban migration, adding to the existing number of residents in towns and cities. This rural-urban migration is usually attributed to factors such as declining agricultural growth and production, causing the displacement and eviction of farmers; floods and natural calamities are also push factors. The lure of urban areas is the availability of jobs in industry and services, the desire for better schooling and health facilities, aspirations to join an urban culture and the 'bright lights' phenomenon.

It is at this point that inequality develops. Upper- income groups are able to form housing cooperatives along community and professional lines, obtaining land from the state at subsidized rates, mobilizing private resources, arranging site development and allotting plots to members at low prices. In contrast, lower-income groups lack the power of organization and have tended to squat on vacant state land and, in some cases, even privately owned land. This is the reason behind *'katchi abadis* (squatter settlements)'. In most cases, these are located on the outskirts of the city or on environmentally unsafe land, where health, sanitation and sewerage facilities are particularly poor.

Various housing programmes have been initiated at government level, although their results have not turned out to be very encouraging. The first 5-year plan in Pakistan (1955–60) allocated about 11 per cent of total plan outlay to physical planning and housing (Economic Watch 2003). But in successive five-year plans the allocation for this sector was greatly reduced; the minimum being 5 per cent allocated in the third five-year plan.

The fifth and sixth five-year plans completely ignored the housing sector. It was in the seventh five-year plan that provision for housing and other service facilities for lower and middle-income groups had some real presence. An ambitious target was set of 2.2 million seven *marla* (1907.22 sq ft) plots in rural areas, which was over-achieved as far as the allotments were concerned (Economic Watch 2003). However, most of the schemes were in inaccessible areas and remained unutilized. By the eighth five-year plan, the government effectively abdicated its role in housing provision, which is evident from the reduction in the allocation for physical planning and housing to a mere 0.9 per cent of total development outlay (Economic Watch 2003). A five-point programme was then launched in December 1985 for the period 1988–90 (Economic Watch 2003). It was claimed that the successful implementation of this programme would dramatically change the socio-economic conditions of the masses, especially the poor, and usher in a quiet revolution in rural areas. However, very sadly, the programme was suspended one year later after Rs 117 million (US$1.6 million) had been spent.

In short, the inept housing policies of different governments have resulted in a housing backlog of over eight million houses, increasing by 300,000 every year. (HRCP 2012). Southern Pakistan suffered from floods for the third year in a row in 2010 and millions of people were affected. The floods damaged or destroyed at least 275,720 houses in 2012 alone (HRCP 2012).

Conclusions

Today Pakistan stands at a crossroads, with multiple threats of economic and political imbalance. Underdevelopment, poor social indicators, an uncontrollable law and order situation, the militarization of state and society, drug trafficking, ethnic and sectarian violence, child abuse and violence against women and minorities are the highlight issues. The situation regarding education, health and housing is dismal.

Because of weak civil society and the absence of viable political or socio-cultural organizations rooted in the masses, the unaccountability of the state has only added to its inability to deal with pressing economic, political and social issues. This circumstance has adversely affected the citizens of Pakistan, especially poor people, women, children and minorities.

On the economic front, the country is continually in a state of dilapidation due to structural problems, a domestic energy crisis, the decline in investment, persistent high inflation and security issues. The budget deficit and losses by state-owned enterprises remain high compared to tax revenue. Due to electricity and gas shortages and security issues, gross fixed investment has also declined.

Poverty is continually increasing, with 58.7 million out of a total population of 180 million subsisting below the poverty line. This includes more than half the population in remote Balochistan, 33 per cent in Sindh and 32 per cent in Khyber Pakhtunkhwa. The lack of meaningful, non-discriminatory representation of all provinces in decision-making has added to the poverty in the above provinces. Inequitable resource distribution among the provinces has been a major cause of ethnic conflict and has strengthened terrorist groups in the remote areas of Khyber Pakhtunkhwa and Balochistan.

To conclude, the state has failed to deliver in almost all important areas of development necessary for a decent life for the majority of people in Pakistan. This does not call merely for the restructuring of the state and its policies but for enhanced efforts on the part of civil society and the corporate sector to contribute significantly to the broader public good. Although the failure of the state to deliver has resulted in social and political conflicts that are the root cause of the threat to economic and social development, after the state only corporations have the essential component resources to achieve equitable development in Pakistan. Thus, it seems only appropriate that this sector should play an active role in this direction. The sector is already donating millions through philanthropic and charitable work. What is important is to organize corporate giving on the lines of modern CSR concepts.

4 Industrial development, management culture and CSR in Pakistan

The extent of the CSR movement depends on the evolution and strength of the corporate sector in society. There is a direct link between a thriving private sector developed along modern lines and the nature of CSR in any country. A weak and underdeveloped corporate sector operated through centralized and weak management systems would not generate a healthy CSR movement. This chapter examines the history and current state of industrial-sector development in Pakistan, its management culture and the outlook for corporate contributions to development in Pakistan.

As will be shown in later chapters, the nature of CSR in Pakistan is still philanthropic, based on charitable giving. Nevertheless, the amount of corporate giving in Pakistan is phenomenal. According to the Pakistan Center for Philanthropy, only publicly listed companies in Pakistan donated Rs 3.8 billion (US$36 million) in 2012; this is an increase of nearly seventeenfold from Rs 228 million in 2000. Overall, too, charitable giving in Pakistan is on the rise. Currently, Pakistan leads South Asia in charitable giving. The major chunk of corporate giving, however, is untapped by development NGOs. Moreover, corporate giving has yet to be fully institutionalized and most decisions around giving are taken by companies' owners and their families.

Pakistan is an agrarian society in which 64 per cent of the population lives in rural areas. The economy, therefore, and people's livelihoods are mainly tied to agriculture. The corporate sector is mainly engaged in commodity production and services. The industrial sector comprises manufacturing, construction, mining and quarrying, electricity generation and distribution, and gas distribution. Similarly, the sectors involved in the service industry are transport, storage and communication, wholesale and retail trade, general government services, and housing services (GoP 2013). Although small and medium-size companies dominate the industrial scene, 80 per cent of the revenue of the private sector comes from large national and multinational companies that also include large public sector organizations and 20 per cent from small and medium companies.

Pakistan's industrial sector is weak, 'dependent on state patronage, and prone to structural deficiencies' (Ali & Malik 2009: 1). The manufacturing sector is not diverse; it relies on textiles that have suffered low profitability in the past few years. Total investment in the private sector has declined from 18.79 per cent of GDP in 2006/7 to 14.22 per cent of GDP in 2012/13 (ESoP 2013). Accompanied by falling investment, the overall performance of the already weak industrial sector was affected by devastating floods and rains which exacerbated the general economic conditions, the deteriorating law and order situation, internal security hazards and the energy crisis. A deteriorating power sector is the main constraint on industrial growth. Due to the above reasons, the share of the manufacturing sector in GDP declined from 14.4 per cent in 2007/8 to 13.2 per cent in 2012/13 (ESoP 2013). The global financial crisis further stunted the growth of the industrial sector in Pakistan. Growth in the manufacturing sector declined from 6.1 per cent in 2010 to 3.4 in 2012. Growth in the mining sector increased from 4.5 per cent in 2009/10 to 7.6 per cent in 2012/13 (ESoP 2013).

Ali & Malik (2009: 2) have argued that:

> Existing research on this subject has tended to locate these failures in policy errors since the first attempt at industrialization in the 1960s that proved to be short-lived, and how nationalization of industry in the 1970s hampered the growth of corporate sector in Pakistan. The problem is not couched in an historical and political economy perspective.

It is imperative, therefore, to outline a history of industrial development in political economy perspective and the corporate management culture it has generated as well as how the outlook developed through such a management culture has influenced the way the corporate sector is involved in CSR in Pakistan.

As in the Indian subcontinent generally, in Pakistan the capitalist mode of production in agriculture and industry was introduced by the British colonial administration (Gardezi 1983). However, as observed by Gardezi (1983: 29):

> It should be noted that by the middle of the nineteenth century, when modern capitalist relations of production were being introduced in Pakistan, feudalism had already ended in England and the capitalist class had established exclusive control over the domestic economy and the state power. In Pakistan, by contrast, pre-capitalist formations were still strong, although no one mode of production was clearly dominant. The British colonial administration introduced capitalist relations selectively in the region, but always in subservice to the imperial interest of the mother country.

Alavi (1983) calls the above mode of production the colonial mode of production. Moreover, in all regions of Pakistan the British systematically strengthened feudal relations of production in the primary sector of the economy. They shattered the pre-colonial economy without adequately replacing it with a viable capitalist mode based on business and commerce (Gardezi 1983).

One of the major interventions of the British was to give permanent property rights to groups loyal to them across the Indian subcontinent through the Permanent Settlement Act. This gave birth to what Kosambi calls 'feudalism from below'. In this connection Kosambi (1975) differentiates between two distinct stages of feudalism in the subcontinent: 1) feudalism from above, and 2) feudalism from below. The pre-colonial era of 'feudalism from below' refers to a tributary system of taxation, in which communities were supposed to provide part of their surplus produce to the king as tribute through government servants who were allowed to govern small territories. When necessary they could be transferred to other territories at the will of the king. The 'feudalism from below' in the colonial era refers to a class of permanent feudal lords who directly controlled the land given to them as property.

In this connection, the British government provided vast tracks of land to several agrarian groups belonging to agricultural castes and a number of civilian and military personnel loyal to the British. The loyalty of these groups was important for local support on a long-term basis and for the continuous flow of revenues from agricultural production (Ali 1987, 1988). The extensive land settlement schemes for the dominant agrarian groups were later accompanied by a canal irrigation network in the subcontinent that was the largest in the world. In short, the colonial law of permanent settlement created a class of feudal lords in Pakistan to the detriment of the majority of landless poor farmers.

The conversion of land into private property did allow market forces to come into play within an agrarian economy, but this did not result in the accumulation of commercial or industrial capital to any significant degree (Gardezi 1983). The British introduced a modern infrastructure in the form of railways, communications, banking and trade to boost capitalism, but this remained tied to mostly feudal relations of production (Gardezi 1983). Moreover, the British neglected the industrial sector in the areas that became Pakistan. In 1947 the industrial sector was virtually non-existent in the country (Gardezi 1983).

In 1947, therefore, due to a weak industrial base, industry contributed a mere 1 per cent of the national income. Pakistan was largely composed of the least economically developed territories of India – those with the pronounced features of an agrarian economy of the colonial type, i.e. specializing in the production of agricultural raw materials, in this case primarily jute and cotton. Out of a total of 14,569 industrial enterprises in undivided India at partition in 1947, Pakistan ended up with only 146, or 9.6 per cent (Nadeem 1970: 10). Most of these were small cottage or semi-cottage industries for the primary processing of agricultural raw material; there were practically no machine-manufacturing means of production (GoP 1949). Only 10 per cent of the known mineral deposits and 5.3 per cent of the energy resources of undivided India went to Pakistan (Malik 2009). Moreover, 'Pakistan had to pay for the upkeep of its defense forces, build an administrative structure and resettle the millions fleeing into its territories' (Jalal 1990: 33).

Although, Muslim mercantilists from the industrially developed part of India did migrate to Pakistan to further their fortunes, they did not have the political voice of feudal lords, tribal leaders and the civil and military bureaucracy. The weak mercantile class, therefore, lacking political voice and representation, was hardly in a position to take over the administration from colonial powers at the time of the partition of the Indian subcontinent.

Due to its weak economy and limited industrial base, industrial growth became a major policy concern for the state of Pakistan in the first two decades. The underlying fear was whether Pakistan would survive as an independent state, given the spectre of Indian domination (Alavi 1983). However, despite the government's incentives, the private sector – primarily based on mercantilism – was slow to move into industry in the early years (Alavi 1983). Between 1950 and 1960, especially during the boom years of the Korean War, trading was more profitable (Ali & Malik 2009). The Korean War 'led to large increases in the prices of raw materials in foreign markets. Since trading had become so profitable in this period, the government introduced a more liberal trade policy; the newly established Pakistani trading classes benefited greatly' (Ali & Malik 2009: 38).

The Korean War boom led to the emergence of a large group of traders in Pakistan (Ali & Malik 2009). However, the end of the Korean War precipitated a long-term foreign exchange crisis that made it unviable for the government to 'pursue a liberal import policy' (Alavi 1983: 48). The above predicament led mercantilists to show some interest in industrial development (Alavi 1983: 48). The government of Pakistan responded to this new interest and established the Pakistan Industrial Development Corporation (PIDC) in 1950 (Tearle 1965: 227), which started functioning in 1952 (Alavi 1983: 48). The aim of the PIDC was to promote industrial development and 'hive off companies initiated by it to private enterprise when they became commercially viable' (Tearle 1965: 227). However, industrialization was pursued at the expense of agricultural growth. The trend was already evident by 1949/50: national income rose by 37 per cent and manufacturing's share doubled, while agriculture's share correspondingly declined (Power 1963: 195).

The industrial class in Pakistan did not evolve naturally but through state patronage. Moreover, industrial capitalism developed within the 'framework of elaborate bureaucratic controls which, far too often, had little intrinsic justification' (Alavi 1983: 49). This was a colonial legacy, as the colonial powers had endeavoured to control industry and restrict industrial growth, as witnessed in India during World War II (Alavi 1983: 49). Alavi (1983) argues that such controls had no justification in independent Pakistan, but the government not only retained but extended such controls. Elaborating further, Alavi (1983: 49) states:

> In fact, the controls became so numerous and complicated that at one stage the government had to set up an Investment Promotion Bureau to act as a clearing house for information for businessmen, and to guide

them through the minefield of restrictions that they had to overcome, and the permits and licenses that they had to obtain in order to carry on.

The above enabled the bureaucracy to tighten its grip over business ventures. This led to increasing corruption in the form of large-scale bribery (Alavi 1983). The result was not only conspicuous consumption by bureaucrats but also money generated by corrupt business transactions, either via partnerships with other businessmen or by companies using the name of spouses or close relatives (Alavi 1983). Due to the dominance of bureaucracy, in a short time those families with a close relationship to influential bureaucrats became the most important business entrepreneurs (Alavi 1983). Due to this state of affairs, the key to success for businessmen was access to government channels (Ali & Malik 2009). Smaller businessmen who did not have access to government channels and did not have the resources to adequately grease the palm of bureaucrats were left out. Moreover, state bodies such as PIDC had an inclination to support larger enterprises that offered good security and higher profits, Ali & Malik's (2009: 39) comment is instructive in this regard:

> The Pakistan Industrial Development Corporation (PIDC) was believed to have favored established industrial families. The Adamjee family, which emerged as the biggest industrial house at the end of the 1950s and established a dominant position in the jute industry, was said to have achieved this position through association with the PIDC. Other leading business families like the Saigol, Ispahani, Amin and Crescent groups were also major beneficiaries.

State patronage of business resulted in a government-business relationship that was based, according to Kochanek (1983), on individual rather than collective action. The demands businessmen made on the government were individual rather than collective. In other words, the emphasis was on the fulfilment of personal needs, not the reform of broad policies (Kochanek 1983). Businessmen's access to senior as well as junior government officials required a highly complex system of personal contacts (Kochanek 1983). Without such contacts, benefits could not be secured. Kochanek (1983) further explains that collective action was largely ceremonial in nature and, though business associations existed, using them to deal with the government was infrequent and had weak roots. State governance was highly centralized and coercive, and decision-makers, as the patrons of business, had an enormous advantage when it came to silencing any opposition (Kochanek 1983). Such a state of affairs hindered the establishment of an effective relationship between business and society. Business in Pakistan did not have any roots in society. This was particularly evident in the 1970s when the government of the late Zulfiqar Ali Bhutto nationalized major industries without any significant political opposition led by the business community.

When the capital of Pakistan was shifted from Karachi to Islamabad by Ayub Khan, the discourse around liaison and lobbying with government officials became more complex (Kochanek 1983). Most companies established liaison offices in Islamabad staffed by two or three people. They were given substantial funds for entertainment and were known for throwing lavish parties for senior government officials (Kochanek 1983). During the military regime of Ayub Khan, several retired military officials were hired by these companies to establish connections with the military bureaucracy to get maximum benefit from the state. Rizvi (1976: 149, as cited in Kochanek 1983: 254) in this context states:

> The retired military officers emerged as a class occupying the top posts of public and private enterprises. The military became a ladder of respectable jobs in the society. A good number of retired Lieutenant-Generals, Major Generals and Brigadiers, and their equivalent ranks in the other services were provided with top positions in government and semi-government companies, autonomous bodies and boards, where they could draw handsome salaries and other facilities admissible under the terms and conditions of service. Various private firms and limited companies offered them directorships to avail of their influence and contacts in their dealings with the government some of the senior military officers resigned their posts to take up some of the positions mentioned above.

In short, unlike the bourgeoisie in India, which had a political voice in society and was therefore was not a supplicant to the government, the nascent industrial class in Pakistan, lacking such roots, was at the mercy of state bureaucracy. The case of state intervention in Pakistan was also different from that of 'tiger' economies, where developmentally driven economic bureaucracies were highly competent, powerful and insulated from the pressures of interest groups in society. The relative autonomy of political and bureaucratic elites was a major factor behind the rapid economic and industrial growth of these countries. Relative autonomy in this context means state independence from the demands of special interests (whether class, regional or sectoral) (Leftwich: 1995). In other words, relative autonomy means the ability of the state to stand above special interests for the sake of national interest (Leftwich: 1995). In the case of Pakistan, none of the characteristics of tiger economies were present. A competent economic bureaucracy insulated from the demands of interest groups hardly existed. On the contrary, it was the military elite and their interests that dominated the state's economic policies in and after Ayub Khan's regime.

Pakistan's early industrial development in the 1950s was based on import-substituting industrialization under tariff barriers and an overvalued exchange rate (Khan 1999). In the 1960s, during Ayub Khan's military regime, however, industrial strategies evolved into a more coherent industrial policy (Khan 1999). Ayub subsidized industrial credit and its allocation was controlled by two state-owned industrial banks (Khan 1999). Moreover, state enterprises were set up that were later sold to the private sector. Incentives were offered to exporters under a 'bonus voucher' scheme to promote exports (Khan 1999). Earlier controls were abandoned and trade was liberalized.

Through the bonus voucher scheme, market forces determined the provision of foreign exchange. It was not provided at the official rate of exchange (Kochanek 1983). The outcome of such a policy was less profit for merchants involved in international trade and a reduction of their potential investment capital (Kochanek 1983). Moreover, industry was established in different provinces, which enabled state governors to use industrial licenses as a political tool to support their favourites. The 'combined effect of these two policies, according to Burki, was to broaden the base of the entrepreneurial sector in Pakistan' (Kochanek 1983: 78).[1]

Though industrialization was encouraged and Ayub's period saw a significant increase in industrial growth, the top-down industrialization initiated by the state through regulation and control led to the concentration of industry in the hands of a few Muslim business families (known as monopoly houses), which were previously involved in trade (Kochanek 1983). The chief economist of the Planning Commission during Ayub's regime, Mahbub-ul-Haq, is known for referring to the monopoly of 'twenty-two-families' owning 87 per cent of banking and insurance and 66 per cent of the industrial assets in the country during that time (Rashid 1983). In this connection, Rashid (1983: 247) has argued that:

> A study on the concentration of industrial assets would be incomplete if we did not take into account the control of the industrial houses over the banking and insurance sector in the country. The very close link between financial and industrial capital is one of the pertinent features of the growth of capitalism in the country, as it played a very important role in establishing the position of the industrial houses and an even more important one in their being able to maintain it.

It was not only the banking and insurance sectors that were controlled by the dominant business families; they also had a significant influence over government-controlled financial institutions (Ali & Malik 2009). This was because they sat on the board of a number of the government's financial institutions, such as PICIC, the principal foreign aid loan-disbursing agency in the country (Ali & Malik 2009). Seven leading monopoly houses were represented on the board of PICIC, while one of them, Adamjee, was chair. Almost 65 per cent of total loans disbursed by PICIC from its inception in 1958 until 1970 went to 37 monopoly houses, with 13 of the larger monopoly houses getting 70 per cent of this.

The accumulation of wealth among a few families created even greater inequality between the rich and the poor. This inequality was defended by the economic planners. For example, Mahbub-ul-Haq justified it in the following words:

> It is well to recognize that economic growth is a brutal, sordid process. There are no short cuts to it. The essence of it lies in making the laborer produce more than he is allowed to consume for his immediate needs, and to invest and reinvest the surplus thus obtained … . What is important and intellectually honest is to admit frankly that the heart of the growth problem lies in maximizing the creation of this surplus. Either the capitalist sector should be allowed to perform the role or if this is found inefficient because of the nature of the capitalist sector in a particular country or is distasteful, the State should undertake it. It would be wrong to dub the consequent emergence of surplus as exploitation: it is justification of economic growth.
>
> (Haq 1963, as cited in Gardezi & Rashid 1983: 10)

Such an outlook created unrest within the labouring class, while increasing regional inequalities led to an anti-Ayub movement in 1968/69 (Kochanek 1983). An antagonistic anti-business sentiment was developed and 'almost every political group in Pakistan advocated a major change in government policies towards the private sector and especially against the alleged twenty-two families' (Kochanek 1983: 79).

Moreover, according to Ali (2001), the rural hierarchy – having a political voice and representation – was also not happy when some of the dominant business families expanded their business within a short span of time through trade and induced industrialization. Rural hierarchy 'presumably had good grounds for dissatisfaction with the expansion of big business. Agricultural growth rates had stagnated since the 1950s, accompanied by negligible state expenditure on agricultural development' (Ali 1987).

Under the above conditions, Zulfiqar Ali Bhutto launched a mass movement against Ayub's regime. After coming to power, he sought to consolidate his support among the rural poor and urban labouring classes through land reform and the nationalization of industry and financial institutions (Talbot 2009). In 1972 he nationalized over thirty large business concerns in sectors such as engineering, automobiles, chemicals and cement, followed by the nationalization of the financial sector with the takeover of banks and insurance companies in 1973. According to Ali (2001: 115):

> The PPP government went even further. It undertook the extreme measure of nationalizing major part of the intermediate agro-process sector. Rice, flour and edible oil mills were taken over in the hope of serving, at a stroke, entrepreneurial control over the forward linkages of the agricultural value chain. This policy was probably designed to placate the larger landowners, whose agents and representatives now gained hold of these plants.

The nationalization of the important industrial and financial sectors negatively affected big business families, while the nationalization of the edible oil industry affected small entrepreneurs as well. These entrepreneurs had supported the Pakistan People's Party (PPP) movement in 1970 (Talbot 2009). All this was done in the name of Islamic socialism to eliminate poverty and inequality in Pakistan.

After 1975, the trading community withheld its support for the PPP, and even actively opposed it during the agitation of 1977 (Ali 2001). Finally, Zia-ul-Haq denationalized these agro-processing units. The restructuring of the 'state trading corporations was much more retarded: they were to outlast Zia himself' (Ali 2001: 117).

It might be argued that business has failed to recover from these adverse impacts on its potentiality for development. The larger business groups almost completely ceased to develop into modern corporate structures with diversified portfolios (Ali 2001). There was also a failure to introduce a decentralized management culture to companies in Pakistan. Instead, a kinship-based family-orientated business structure still prevails. In addition, 'the major business groups relapsed back into medium-sized family operations' (Ali 2001: 116). Bhutto's nationalization created obstacles for the development of technologically advanced capital-intensive industries and, unlike capital-intensive industrial units internationally, industry in Pakistan has not developed significantly to date (Ali & Malik 2009).

Overall, the underdevelopment of the corporate sector in Pakistan is the result of various factors, including: the political and economic dominance of the military; socially, the dominance of feudal/tribal/agrarian classes accompanied by feudal and agrarian social values; and the lack of a political voice of the business class. These factors together gave birth to a certain national culture that in turn has influenced management culture in the corporate sector in Pakistan. Such a culture failed to innovate new value systems within the corporate sector. All this has a significant influence on the way in which corporate management culture influences CSR in Pakistan, an analysis of which will now follow.

Management culture and CSR in Pakistan

Pakistani business follows a family-orientated, centralized management culture and there are important economic reasons for this (Ali 2001). Compared to multinational companies, Pakistani business 'is composed of family firms in which equity is closely integrated with operations' (Ali 2001: 118). The owner-operator mode, which suits small and medium firms, has been dominant in large enterprises as well (Ali 2001: 118). Due to the dominance of family firms, 'there has been little or no transition towards the building of corporatized business structures or towards "managerial capitalism"' (Ali 2001: 118). Organizational innovation remained dormant.

There are several reasons for this lack of organizational innovation. Ali's (2001: 118–19) analysis in this context is instructive:

> The traumatic setbacks of the 1970s could have impeded this process, the seeds of which might well have sprouted in the 1960s. The culture of business might also be too personalized, acting against instituting systems and decentralized operations. Tax evasion, and the ubiquity of the black economy, has worked against devolving authority to managerial cadres. The insufficient supply of good quality managerial personnel could be another disincentive, though this could be a function also of low compensation levels offered by Pakistan business to managers compared to multinational companies. Even the larger capitalist preferred to establish distinct companies for separate projects or industrial unites, rather than develop divisionalized entities with multiple managerial layers.

Another important reason according to Ali (2001) for an underdeveloped business structures has been the nature of the manufacturing process involved in cotton textiles, which is Pakistan's major industry. Higher volumes of 'production in this industry fail to achieve discernible economies of scale, which would make larger business organizations economically competitive' (Ali 2001: 119) and consequently the textiles industry remained highly fragmented. Furthermore, the phenomenon of family-based equity 'has also prevented any learning curves through horizontal integration' (Ali 2001: 119).

Most importantly, the founding families of large public limited companies have retained their majority equity shares and their transactions in the stock market are largely inactive (Ali 2001). The major motivation to go for public listing was probably to fulfill the requirements of the government in order to acquire highly subsidized project loans from public sector financial institutions rather than opting for corporatized operations (Ali 2001). The result is a family-orientated, centralized corporate culture. Individual businessmen or families continue to take major corporate decisions and enjoy privileges through their access to state functionaries (Ali 2001). Such a management culture has important bearings on corporate giving and the underdevelopment of corporate social responsibility within the indigenous corporate sector in Pakistan.

Organizational culture is not a product of an organization; it comes from people who are influenced by events outside the organization (Khilji 2003). In this connection, work-related 'values and attitudes, such as power distance, tolerance for ambiguity, honesty, pursuance of group or individual goals, work ethic and entrepreneurial spirit, have been argued to be part of the cultural identity of a nation' (Tayeb 1995: 590) and influence the management culture and the culture of corporate social responsibility.

Culture means a collective way of life, or 'the learned and shared ways of thinking and acting among a group of people or a society' (Islam 2004: 311, 312). Culture influences our daily lives and the way we manage organizations and solve problems (Islam 2004). Most anthropologists and sociologists, according to Islam (2004), have argued that culture is acquired and not genetically transferred. It is through culture that human beings adapt to their constantly changing environment. It influences the way people think and behave in different societies. Resultantly, 'the pattern of shared basic assumptions continues to be shared and developed among a given group – a corporate entity, a region or a country' (Islam 2004: 312).

Regarding what is meant by national culture, definitions in the literature abound. In the narrowest sense, the term is used to denote 'a set of historically evolved, learned and shared values, attitudes and meanings' (Khilji 2003: 114). In the wider sense, however, 'the term 'nation' does not only refer to culture but also to all social, economic and political institutions that have a significant bearing on the management of organizations located in a particular environment' (Tayeb 2001, as cited in Khilji 2003: 114).

There have been a number of studies published on the link between an organization and socio-cultural norms. Some authors, according to Tayeb (1995: 590), 'have emphasized universality and similarities between organizations (e.g. Kerr *et al.* 1952; Cole 1973; Hickson *et al.* 1974; Form 1979; Negandhi 1979, 1985), and some others the uniqueness of organizations given their cultural contexts (e.g. Meyer and Rowan 1977; Hofstede 1980; Lincoln *et al.* 1981; Laurent 1983)'.

In this connection, Tayeb (1995: 590) identifies two major approaches: 1) the American institutionalist perspective, and 2) the British contextual perspective. According to the institutionalist perspective, 'organizations cannot be separated from the societies within which they operate, and stress social conformity so emphatically upon organizations that idiosyncrasy and resistance tend to get excluded' (Tayeb 1995: 590). The contextualists, however, profess that organizations can deviate from societal norms (Tayeb 1995: 590). The emphasis of the institutional perspective is on the importance of social rather than just economic aspects of a company. Citing Meyer and Rowan (1977) and DiMaggio and Powell (1983), Tayeb (1995: 590) argues that 'the contribution of institutional theory has been to highlight the importance of social, rather than just economic rationalities for organizations'.

The view that organizational culture is not universal but relative proposes that management systems and the discourse of decision-making (whether centralized or decentralized) differ in different societies because of variations in national cultures. Such variations affect innovation and the international competitiveness of companies as well. In this connection, Tayeb (1995) compares Japan with Iran. She calls Japan competitive and Iran non-competitive. She argues that the competitiveness in Japanese industries such as electronics and car manufacturing is because the country as a whole is competitive and successful; otherwise, these industries would not be that competitive. Iran on the other hand does not possess any internationally competitive industries and relies on the export of crude oil, which is a finite national resource and does not fall into this category. She further makes a comparison between India and Japan and states:

The Japanese societal mix, of harmonious industrial relations, highly educated and skilled workforce and a relative cultural homogeneity and a sense of collective identity, has enabled the managers to capitalize on and incorporate their employees' collectivism in their management practices, such as flexible working arrangements, quality circles and collective decision making (ringi). In India, a societal mix of confrontational industrial relations, cultural heterogeneity and inter-communal hatred and conflicts, a rigid caste system, corruption in certain quarters, massive poverty and a high rate of illiteracy, especially among manual workers, has diminished the managers' ability to transform their collectivist employees into a highly committed workforce who would consider their company as part of their in-group and who would put the interests of their company before theirs. As a result, such practices as quality circles and flexible working arrangements are beyond the reach of most Indian managers.

(Tayeb 1995: 594)

Furthermore, Khilji (2003) while citing Kanungo & Mendonca (1994), argues that in Indian organizations the selection, promotion and transfer of employees is determined by political and familial connections. Interpersonal relations influence job-related decisions rather than merit or suitability. Decision-making is highly centralized and subordinates are expected to accept the decisions of their bosses; 'effective motivational tools are more likely to be social, interpersonal and spiritual' (Budhwar 2001, as cited in Khilji 2003: 111).

With reference to Pakistan, Khilji (2003) identifies four major influences on the country's national culture that in turn affect the culture of human resource management. Her analysis, however, seems to be relevant to the organizational culture in general in the corporate sector as well. Following Khilji (2003), an analysis of management culture and its influence on CSR in Pakistan is in order.

Khilji (2003: 114) argues that Pakistani national culture 'is an amalgam of Islamic religion, Indian origins, British inheritance and American Influence'. Since Pakistan is comprised of four different provinces, with different cultures and languages, the notion of 'national culture' might be questionable. However, in the light of the above-mentioned influences on organizational culture, it can be argued that the sum of such influences might be evident in organizational culture in urban localities in Pakistan. Following Khilji (2003), the paragraphs below provide an analysis of the relevance of each of these influences in understanding organizational culture and practices and their influence on CSR in Pakistan.

The influence of Islamic religion has some bearing on the organizational culture. Although 96 per cent of the Pakistani population is Muslim (GoP 2012), the interpretation of religion by different religious sects makes it difficult to make any generalization about people's attitudes towards Islam (Khilji 2003). However, despite the absence of any single understanding of Islam, religion seems to be important in the lives of Pakistanis. In this connection Khilji (2003: 114, 115) states:

> Assumptions about religion seem to be prominent in the minds of people because the creation of Pakistan emerged from the belief that Muslims of the Indian subcontinent are a separate nation based on their religion and their Islamic cultural heritage. Consequently, they should be given the independence to form their own state in which they could freely practice Islam and formulate systems that would emanate from the teachings of Holy Quran.

However, until General Zia-ul-Haq's military regime, religion remained confined to the private domain. Though lip service was paid to the importance of Islam, it never became part of the public domain. General Zia-ul-Haq, however, endeavoured to move Islam from the private domain to institutionalization at state level. In 1979 he introduced four *Shariat* laws prescribing traditional Islamic punishments. These laws pertained to drinking, adultery, theft and false allegations (Malik 2001). Moreover, he instituted a *Shariat* bench in every high court. These *Shariat* courts had the power to declare any law repugnant to the injunctions of Islam (Malik 2001). Later, in 1980, the Federal Shariat Court (FSC), which included five judges and the chairman and also three ulema (religious scholars), replaced the earlier *Shariat* benches (Malik 2001).

In the economic field, Zia-ul-Haq introduced the Zakat and Ushr Ordinance in 1980. According to this ordinance, the government could deduct *zakat* (charity) at the rate of 2.5 per cent from bank deposits, savings accounts, deposit accounts and shares held by the Muslim population (Malik 2001). In the banking sector, interest-based accounts were replaced by profit-and-loss sharing accounts. Interest was substituted by mark-up. In practice, however, both mark-up and profit were treated by the people as interest, simply renamed (Malik 2001).

Following Tayeb (1997), due to the legacy of the continuous promotion and later institutionalization of Islam in the public sector, religion will have influenced the organizational culture. However, Khilji (2003) argues that the influence of Islamization extends to only a limited degree to organizations. Nevertheless, increasing religiosity has been observable since 2003 due to the so-called American 'war against terror', which created anti-American sentiment in Pakistan. Furthermore, an increasingly deteriorating law and order situation, kidnappings (especially of people with money), and economic uncertainly have significantly created a sense of insecurity in Pakistan and this has added to religious sentiment. It therefore seems that religion is now having a greater influence on organizational culture and the culture of corporate giving in Pakistan.

Khilji (2003) identifies Indian origins as another important factor influencing the organizational culture in Pakistan, and this is clearly visible in the ways that corporate organizations are managed. However, it can be argued that making a case for the influence of Indian culture on Pakistan is a misnomer. First, there is no single Indian culture. The cultures in south and north India, for example, are very different. Second, Pakistan itself is part of the Indian subcontinent. What it would be appropriate to refer to regarding the cultural influences of the Indian subcontinent is the kinship- and honour-based culture prevalent throughout India and Pakistan.

Waseem (1994: 93) argues that 'the primary loyalties of caste/*biradari* (extended family/clan) and tribe as well as tenurial relations serve as political resources of immense significance in Pakistan and channel the political activity in favour of those who command these resources'. It is true for corporate organizations as well, in which caste/*biradari* loyalties hold sway in terms of recruitments and rewards. *Biradari* may be understood to be patrilineal kin (Alvi 2001). Lieven (2011) has argued that kinship is central to society and politics in Pakistan – an important factor responsible for the weakness of the state and an essential force that resists any radical reform or revolution. His argument is equally pertinent with regard to the corporate sector that, because of the domination of families and their *biradari* networks, is unable to institutionalize according to modern norms and is insulated against innovation or radical reform. Islam (2004: 322) notes that:

> These kinship structures are so strong that they extend to towns and cities, penetrating the corporations, public bureaucracy and the political system. The individual is closely integrated into these networks and they determine his/her status, mobility and success. Family networks are the primary focus of loyalty. Their strength is reinforced by endogamous, cross-cousin marriages. The latter enable the family to retain land and assets within the family and build clan networks. These institutions impose a system of mutual obligations, which perpetuates patronage and nepotism in government and private enterprises.

Social structures dominated by kinship relations and networks have given rise to a collectivist or socio-centric culture rather than an individualistic culture within corporate organizations. An organization in which individualistic culture pervades the workplace is 'largely contractual or transactional and work is controlled and organized with reference to individuals and assumed economic rationale and self-interest' (Islam 2004: 321). Contrary to this, in collectivist culture, 'the employment relationship is morally based and management of groups is salient with personal relationships prevailing over the task' (Islam 2004: 321).

Another important feature of socio-centric kinship societies is that its members readily accept inequality and power differences. People respect hierarchy and rank in organizations. The degree of tolerance for power distance influences 'the relationship between management and employees, how responsibilities are assigned and how discipline is maintained' (Islam 2004: 317).

In what Hofstede (1991) called 'high power distance' societies in developing countries such as Pakistan, employees respect those in authority and individuals' titles, rank and status carry a lot of weight (Islam 2004: 317). Subordinates seldom express disagreement and feel dependent on their bosses. In such societies, family-based business concerns prefer centralization in organizational structures. The Pakistani corporate sector, which is characterized by the influence of the kinship system and high power distance management systems, follows a hierarchical structure inwhich the father is considered to be head of the family and the eldest son has more say in decision-making than younger sons (Afghan and Wiqar 2007: 8) – or daughters. In family businesses too, unless the father retires, he heads the organization and in case of retirement in most cases, the eldest son succeeds him. Daughters, even the eldest, do not usually succeed the father as they are supposed to eventually leave their parental home after marriage.

According to Khilji (2003: 115), 'family-like ties are also created with persons who are not biological relatives but who are socially integrated into their groups', and 'family/social allegiance is binding and generally takes precedence over rules'. Members in such a system feel obliged to take care of each other. However, the principle is applicable to in-group members, not out-groups, which are treated differently, and harshly (2003: 115). The characteristics of the Pakistani corporate sector make it a classic example of this kinship-based power distance mode of operations.

As will be shown in detail in later chapters, familial ties and centralized management culture is the norm when making decisions regarding corporate giving for charitable purposes. Even in large national companies, it is either CEOs or their families that take decisions for extending support to welfare causes. In addition, in most cases, donations (monetary as well as non-monetary) are given to those they know personally, through their extended family or their employees. This is an outcome of family-based kinship-orientated management systems, in which awareness of the wider context of society necessitating impersonal contributions is largely missing.

The British legacy is the third important factor influencing organizational culture in Pakistan identified by Khilji (2003). One of the most salient features of British colonial rule in the Indian subcontinent was the creation of elite classes (feudal, military and civil servants). Over 'the past few decades, the relatively small, educated elite has increasingly been displaced by an educated middle class, but without bringing an essential change of attitude' (Khilji 2003: 116). These elite classes always follow what Hofstede (1991) called high power distance management. Such elitism has further strengthened the traditional value system in Pakistan, in which commitment and loyalty is traded for merit.

'Commitment and loyalty' is a behavioral aspect determined by societal norms and cultural ideology. Hofstede (1991) clearly discusses the 'loyalty' factor existing in developing societies. In these societies, 'commitment and loyalty is considered as an important dimension of personality trait and never

made contingent to any financial rewards instead considered as moral obligation' (Mahmood 2008: 45). Citing Ouchi (1985), Mahmood (2008) notes
that employees in Japanese companies seek long-term employment, unlike
employees in US companies. This is because of cultural differences which
mean that loyalty and commitment is more rewarded in Japanese companies.
This seems to be true for developing countries such as Pakistan. An addi-
tional factor, however, in a developing country like Pakistan can be that
people tend to stay in an organization for a long period because high unemployment rates and economic uncertainty necessitate the demonstration of
commitment and loyalty. The point confirms Hofstede (1991), where he notes
the high uncertainty element in developing countries.

Jhatial *et al.* (2012), in a recent study, also identify the strong presence of
elitism in the private sector (as well as the public sector and MNCs) in Pakistan.
According to them:

> Respondents in government and private sector organizations strongly
> point out the existence of unfriendly and coercive management style
> whereas MNCs seem slightly better. This finding is coherent with the
> finding of Khilji (2003). Existence of mentoring in government and
> private organizations seemed at low level as 20 and 40 per cent respon-
> dents agree respectively. On the contrary, 80 per cent respondents in
> MNCs agree that they have strong presence of mentoring support from
> their boss and senior colleagues. Majority of respondents in government
> and private sector organizations agreed they experience harassing and
> sadistic attitudes of boss appear whereas respondents in MNCs also
> witnessed presence of such attitudes at workplace. In view of one
> respondent: 'boss considers his office as fiefdom and subordinates as
> subjects'.
>
> (Jhatial *et al.* 2012: 8–9)

Khilji (2003) also identifies American influence, which is generally considered
more democratic and progressive; however, overall it is the deep-rooted
traditions of religion, kinship-based familial relations and entrenched British
colonial management structures that ultimately determine the choice of how
businesses will be managed in Pakistan. Khilji (2003) argues that, despite lip
service, Islam does not have a significant influence on management systems in
Pakistan. Nevertheless, alongside the increasing economic and social insecurity and greater insecurity of life and property since 2003, religion also seems
to play a larger role. Hofstede (1983) has already identified the importance of
religion in corporate culture in developing countries, where one of the
dimensions of management has a 'strong uncertainty avoidance' attitude. In
this regard, he argues that:

> All religions, in some way, make uncertainty tolerable, because they all
> contain a message that is beyond uncertainty, that helps us to accept the

uncertainty of today because we interpret experiences in terms of something bigger and more powerful that transcends personal reality. In strongly Uncertainty Avoiding societies, we find religions, which claim absolute truth and which do not tolerate other religions.

(Hofstede 1983: 83)

Pakistan can surely be categorized as a strong Uncertainty Avoiding society, for which reason Islam does play a role in corporate culture and how businesses are managed.

The weak corporate sector with underdeveloped managerial structure and centralized decision-making has important consequences for the development of CSR in Pakistan. As will be detailed in later chapters, one major consequence is that CSR is frequently equated with corporate philanthropy/charity. Some consider CSR to be simple compliance with the law. This creates a difficulty because top management in many cases is still uncertain about the true meaning of CSR, i.e. the responsibility of the corporate sector to engage actively in an organized manner in development, social justice and human rights issues for the wider development of society, not just in making one-off charitable donations.

The state of CSR in Pakistan is, therefore, still in its infancy. Only a few companies have a CSR strategy, and mostly these are multinationals which follow their own CSR policies and standards. Some indigenous companies have also developed written CSR policies, but the majority, unfortunately, are 'either unaware of the benefits brought by CSR or they feel that even if they do not adopt such policies, they are not in any state of danger' (Waheed 2005). In most cases, companies give charity to end beneficiaries, whether individuals or organizations, on a one-off basis. Religion, specifically Islam, provides a universal context for giving (whether individual or corporate) in Pakistan. As Bonbright & Azfar (2000: 6) state:

> The Quranic concept of *zakat* (charity) evolved in the course of Muslim thought and history as one among the pillars of the practice of the faith, and has given rise to extensive legal literature that elaborates and expresses the diverse interpretations of this common principle among the various Muslim schools of thought and law. *Zakat* is widely understood as the requirement that the prosperous annually give a certain portion of their total wealth, not just their total income, to support the poor. *Zakat* is often considered, therefore, a religious imperative distinct from voluntary giving in its strictest sense. A customary formulation of *zakat* is a mandatory obligation on all Muslims with a minimum level of wealth to give away 2.5 per cent of that wealth. Where *zakat* is directed is ordinarily a matter of personal choice.

In short, whatever motivates (be it compassion, family tradition or something else), giving is accompanied by religious feelings and attitudes.

Whatever people do for others might give them religious satisfaction in the context of *Haqook-ul-Ibad* (rights of other human beings). What is missing, however, in following the notion of *Haqook-ul-Ibad* is the re-interpretation of the concept to suit the requirements of sustainable development today.

The concept of *ijtihad* (innovation) in Islam becomes key in this regard. Progressive Muslims have re-opened the gates of *ijtihad* in order to accommodate their religion to modern society. Following the principles of *ijtihad*, the concept of charity could be transformed into a contemporary notion of corporate giving to fulfill religious obligations as well as fit in with the modern concept of corporate social responsibility.

Conclusions

Pakistan inherited an almost non-existent industrial sector after the partition of the Indian subcontinent in 1947. This is because the British colonial powers developed industry in areas of the subcontinent that became part of India. The Muslim trading castes that migrated to Pakistan and later developed industry under state patronage and state-led industrialization lacked collectivity and failed to develop a political voice. Bhutto's nationalization process further damaged industry and to date the industrial sector has not taken off to the degree witnessed in neighbouring India.

Due to the particular political economy of Pakistan, in which industrialization did not emerge from within society through an organic process but was initiated and controlled by the state, the business class did not develop roots within society. As a result, instead of being able to introduce modern industrial and social values evident in modern industrial societies, it was influenced by a culture dominated by feudal and tribal norms and understandings of religion and the colonial legacy of elitism.

Consequently, the corporate sector remains tied to family-orientated business concerns, fostering a culture of centralized management systems. It has failed to introduce innovative decentralized management or 'managerial capitalism'.

The underdevelopment of the industrial sector and management culture is reflected in the way corporate social responsibility is managed in Pakistan. As will be demonstrated in later chapters, CSR is also managed centrally, by companies' CEOs or their family members. The basic motivation for the corporate elite remains religious and the kinship-based value system is the basic determinant of corporate giving. However, it would be wrong to expect that modern CSR of the Western type can be imported and imposed on the current cultural fabric. CSR has to evolve from the culture and traditions it will inhabit. What would be important is to create awareness in the corporate sector that for whatever reason – whether religion or another – they need to organize their corporate giving so that their resources are not wasted in one-off philanthropic/charity work but might be used for long-term sustainable development. Civil society organizations and the government can play an important role in this. Both can create awareness about modern CSR through their engagement with the corporate sector. Another important role the government can play is to document the economy and control the black economy. Documentation and proper auditing of accounts can lead business people in Pakistan to opt for organized reporting and written CSR policies.

Note

1 Kochanek was citing Javed Burki, a prominent Pakistani economist.

5 Government regulations regarding CSR in Pakistan

Corporate social responsibility is most often considered to be the voluntary activities of corporations for social good. However, in recent years we have witnessed a new trend, in which governments have also started promoting CSR, 'reflecting broader governance trends that embrace "soft law", quasi-voluntary standards, and other novel incentives to move companies toward and beyond minimum regulatory goals' (Ho 2013: 375). This chapter analyzes the role of government in CSR by first providing a rationale for and examples of the role of government in some European and Asian countries and then the contributions of the government of Pakistan in this area.

To begin with, in order to strengthen CSR, governments have joined other stakeholders such as civil society and corporations. According to Albareda *et al.* (2008: 348):

> At the start of the century, these governmental initiatives converged with the actions of different international organizations such as the UN Global Compact and the European Commission, both of which began to promote and endorse CSR, recognizing that the role of public administration and public policy initiatives were key in encouraging a greater sense of CSR.

The growing role of governments is also linked to challenges brought about by globalization and a changing economic environment giving birth to a changing role for business in society, by concepts such as corporate citizenship and the interrelationship between trade, investment and sustainable development (Albareda *et al.* 2008: 348). At the macro level, the primary role of the public sector is to provide an enabling environment in which businesses can undertake CSR efforts as part of their business strategy in the country (Sarmila *et al.* 2013). The 'enabling role played by the government sector would refer to four key roles that are mandating, facilitating, partnering and endorsing' (Fox *et al.* 2002, as cited in Sarmila *et al.* 2013: 18). At the micro level, the government's role is represented by public-private partnerships. The aims of the 'partnership are to share resources, knowledge and capability between business corporations and the government agency' (Sarmila *et al.* 2013: 18).

With reference to governments' role in CSR, Waheed's (2005: 26) important study on CSR in Pakistan makes several suggestions for governments, as cited below:

- Governments should pursue their traditional function of promoting trade and business through a proper policy. Supporting economic growth establishes support for democracy. The strongest foundations for the stability, predictability, and security necessary for a sustainable business environment are democratic governments that protect human rights and labour rights.
- Government must work with companies to promote strong corporate values which promote legal and ethical behaviour as well as respect human rights and labour rights.
- Governments should support and facilitate public-private efforts to promote corporate responsibility bringing seemingly disparate groups together for serious efforts to address mutually recognized problems. The Voluntary Principles and Social Accountability International are two good examples of such efforts.
- Governments should support existing international standards and adopt them in their policies to delegate them to their local businesses making them readily competitive for the international market.
- Governments should help civil society, business, academics, NGOs and unions to join hands together and craft credible solutions for their day to day problems and help them implement that throughout the business chain.
- Governments can promote the CSR agenda through legislation, media and create awards to encourage the organizations to adopt the changes.

With reference to government and CSR in Europe, Albareda *et al.* (2007: 401) have built up a 'four ideals' typology model for European governmental action on CSR: 1) the partnership model, 2) the 'business in the community' model, 3) the sustainability and citizenship model and 4) the Agora model.[1] In the partnership model, adopted by countries such as Denmark, Finland, the Netherlands and Sweden, the government encourages partnership as a strategy shared between sectors (companies, civil society and other associations/social organizations, etc.) for meeting socio-employment challenges (Albareda *et al.* 2007: 401).

In the sustainability and citizenship model adopted by the governments of Ireland and the United Kingdom, soft intervention policies are introduced to encourage companies' involvement in governance challenges affecting the community (Albareda *et al.* 2007: 401). In the sustainability and citizenship model adopted by governments in Germany, Austria, Belgium and Luxembourg, the emphasis is on the 'updated version of the existing social agreement and emphasis on a strategy of sustainable development' (Albareda *et al.* 2007: 401). In the Agora model adopted by France, Italy, Spain, Greece and Portugal, the emphasis is on creating 'discussion groups for the different social actors to achieve public consensus on CSR' (Albareda *et al.* 2007: 401). In short, based on the historical evolution of the relationship between the state, society and business, a range of possibilities exist in relation to government policy and the definition of their role vis-à-vis CSR.

Within the developing world, while the example of Indonesia's mandatory CSR policy is somewhat controversial, the government role in CSR in China is cited in the literature as exemplary. Being the leader among emerging markets, China provides an important example of the state promotion of CSR. China has instituted new measures to promote CSR as an explicit policy objective at various levels over the past decade. Several measures require legal compliance or regulatory mandates, 'others go "beyond regulation" but make use of existing institutions and incentive structures' (Ho 2013: 378). Such initiatives make China one of the leading governments in the world that actively promote CSR. Though China's governmental role vis-à-vis CSR has only recently attracted the attention of Western legal scholars, China is even ahead of many countries in the OECD in this area.

As in other countries in both the North and the South there has been a growing awareness within the public sector in Pakistan of the need to play a role in strengthening CSR. As far back as 2002 the government decided to set up the Pakistan Compliance Initiative Board (PCIB) to facilitate exporters, particularly the small and medium enterprises (SMEs), in meeting such international social compliance standards as ISO-9000, ISO-14000 and SA-8000. The PCIB was established on the recommendation of the private sector to tackle the environmental, labour and other issues that exporters could face on the world market. The board would consist of the representatives of exporters of carpets, textiles, surgical instruments, sports goods, ready-made garments, hosiery, bedwear, etc. Moreover, the ministries of labour, commerce, the interior and environment would also be represented on the board.

The board would create awareness among exporters, especially SMEs, of the importance of attaining social compliance standards in a post-WTO world following the abolition of the quota system in 2005, and – to facilitate buyers – set up a database of certified companies.

The government intended to take steps to encourage private companies to attain internationally recognized social compliance certification to stay in the world market. The abolition of quotas would trigger intense competition, requiring exporters to improve the quality of their goods, become more competitive and comply with international social standards.

In this connection, the Minister of Commerce said, 'It is imperative that Pakistani companies bring their exportable production up to the recognized international standards to stay in business as the buyers would do business only with those who comply with their social standards. Lack of certification can lead to decline in exports and also prove to be a non-tariff barrier against the Pakistani goods' (DAWN: 2002).

The minister's speech was also relevant in the context of international pressure on the manufacturing sector in Pakistan, evident as far back as the 1990s. For example, the exploitation of children in the sports industry in the city of Sialkot, which produces 75 per cent of the world's soccer balls, became a major concern internationally, with serious concerns raised by civil society groups and major buyers in the 1990s. In 1996, international sports goods manufacturers asked the advice of the Save the Children Fund (SCF). However, although the Pakistan Compliance Initiative (PCI) was declared key to national trade policy, not much progress has been seen since its launch in 2003 and the establishment of the PCIB in 2004. Nevertheless, progress in this direction could have positive results in strengthening CSR in Pakistan.

The Companies Ordinance, 1994, overseen by statutory bodies such as the Security Exchange Commission of Pakistan (SECP), regulates the corporate sector in Pakistan. Government-recognized bodies such as trade associations and chambers of commerce represent the business sector's interests (Waheed 2005: 27). Over the past five years, the SECP has approved various guidelines for public limited companies that provide a baseline for organizations to report their CSR activities in their annual report (Khan 2013: 924). In 2009, all public companies were required to comply with the SECP Statuary Notification, disclosing their monetary and descriptive status in their audited and annexed directors' reports (Khan 2013: 924). These companies must disclose their monetary and descriptive status in the audited and annexed directors' report. The areas where they could notify were listed as:

> Corporate philanthropy, energy conservation, environmental protection measures, community investment and welfare schemes, consumer protection measures, welfare spending for under-privileged classes, industrial relations, employment of special persons, occupational safety and health, business ethics and anticorruption measures, national-cause donations, contribution to national exchequer, rural development programs.
>
> (Khan 2013: 924)

Khan (2013) noted that though companies did provide a description of their involvement in the above, they did not include the total spent on all activities. In July 2013, the SECP drafted the Corporate Social Responsibility Guidelines. The basic objective of these guidelines was to promote the development of a framework for CSR initiatives by all companies (SECP 2013). The government has encouraged companies to work in cooperation with stakeholders to implement a transparent and socially responsible business strategy.

The guidelines suggest a CSR governance structure composed of the board of directors of the company committed to socially responsible business. Box 5.1 outlines what the board of directors is required to ensure regarding CSR.

Box 5.1 Guidelines for the board of directors

The board of directors must ensure that:

- CSR policy is incorporated into the vision, code of ethics and business plan/strategy of the company;

- a CSR commitment statement is agreed through meetings/ sessions by the board of directors with reference to CSR definition, business value of CSR, vision and commitment (resources, time, personnel);
- the output of CSR commitment is integrated into a board-level SR policy;
- the CSR mandate is executed either through a pre-existing committee or by forming a new CSR committee;
- education/orientation sessions are held to ensure that board members have adequate understanding of and expertise in CSR for making informed decisions;
- CSR activities are included as part of the agenda of board meetings and CSR included in the annual board evaluation;
- the operations of the board are periodically reviewed to identify and implement measures to align board operations with the company's CSR strategy;
- CSR goals, objectives and targets are incorporated into business plans/strategy;
- board members determine CSR risks, opportunities and impact prior to any major business decisions (acquisition, mergers, product variation, capital expenditures);
- board members review and approve CSR-related communications to internal and external stakeholders ensuring compliance with the relevant reporting framework.

(SECP 2013)

Companies are also encouraged to form a CSR consultative committee ideally led by CSR experts. It is recommended that the committee provides specialized supervision of CSR activities and periodic reporting of the progress of CSR activities to the board of directors (SECP 2013). In order to incorporate CSR into companies' corporate strategies, companies are encouraged to formulate CSR policies paving the way for systematic CSR management systems. Broad indicators given in Box 5.2 are expected to be reflected in the systems.

Box 5.2 Indicators

- Express commitment by the board and top management to formulate and implement CSR policy.
- Ensuring that policies, processes and systems exist and support the CSR policy.

This is measured by:

1. specifying the organizational approach towards CSR;

2. incorporating the CSR approach into the company's code of ethics;
3. defining objectives for carrying out CSR activities;
4. setting targets for the achievement of CSR objectives;
5. determining the working model and devising an action plan (time, resources, budget);
6. delegating responsibility and management of resources with respect to CSR policy.

- Sensitization and training of the board, senior management and employees for implementation of CSR targets
- Mechanism for stakeholder engagement prior, during and on conclusion of CSR plans
- Periodic monitoring and evaluation of CSR activities
- Disclosure and reporting of CSR achievements
- Recognizing and documenting the shortfalls/failures
- Incorporating improvement in future CSR policy/plans

(SECP 2013)

Clear priority areas for support are expected of companies' CSR policies regarding current and future projects. It is recommended (SECP 2013) that the following broad areas be covered:

- Community investment (skill development, livelihood, health, education, infrastructure, social enterprise development, safe drinking water, poverty alleviation, youth development and environment conservation)
- Governance (human rights, transparency, anti-corruption, business practices, stakeholder relations, responsible marketing)
- Product responsibility
- Work-life balance
- Safety (risk management, disaster management)
- Climate change

The CSR policy is expected to be implemented through a systemized structure that measures and reflects progress towards CSR goals/targets. It is imperative that the system be able to identify the role of the company and the extent of involvement of internal and external stakeholders for carrying out CSR plans. The implementation system may indicate the following:

- specific goals, business plan and working model to be implemented;
- resources aligned for implementation of CSR goals;
- the extent of implementation and completion of CSR activities;
- changes incorporated into the working model in response to changes in business/social needs;
- the specific role and resources of partnering agencies;

- systemized periodic assessment of the impact of CSR policy/goals;
- the systematic reporting system regarding the implementation of CSR policies to internal and external stakeholders.

Definite allocation of resources both monetary (a certain percentage of profits) and non-monetary (e.g. allocation of voluntary time or hours of service at a collaborating agency) is expected of companies' CSR policies. The method of allocation of resources or identified criteria should ideally be predetermined, duly endorsed by the board and form part of CSR policy.

To ensure that companies are systematically implementing their CSR policies, the SECP guidelines recommend an external assurance system whereby companies can obtain assurance from external parties. Such assurance is expected to be evidence-based and documented according to defined procedures. Box 5.3 provides details of assurance guidelines.

Box 5.3 Assurance guidelines

Assurance should:
- be conducted by entities, groups or individuals external to the reporting organization, who are demonstrably competent in the subject matter and assurance practices;
- utilize groups or individuals who are not unduly limited by their relationship with the organization or its stakeholders to reach and publish an independent and impartial conclusion on the report;
- be implemented in a manner that is systematic, documented, evidence-based, and characterized by defined procedures;
- assess whether the CSR report of the company provides a reasonable and balanced presentation of performance, taking into consideration the veracity of report data and the overall selection of content;
- assess the extent to which the report preparer has applied any Reporting Framework; and
- result in an opinion or set of conclusions that is publicly available in written form, and a statement from the assurance provider on their relationship to the report preparer.

(SECP 2013)

Finally, the guidelines emphasize CSR reporting, whereby companies are expected to report their CSR policy and activities consolidated in the form of a separate CSR report. Such a report may 'prominently disclose the CSR objectives, working model, implementation status, impact/achievements, risks, opportunities, challenges and working partners. This may also include comparison drawn from the previous year' (SECP 2013: 6). The SECP (2013: 6) also recommends that:

- CSR reporting is expected to state the goals that the board has planned to set forth for the next year. This may be descriptive narration of the areas of concentration or any specific projects along with brief overview of source of generation of funds for said goals.
- Companies are expected to prominently disclose CSR report (summarized or detailed format). The said reports may be disseminated on its website (if any), annual reports, separate report and other communication media.
- Notwithstanding the preparation of CSR Report, the company shall provide descriptive as well as monetary disclosures of the CSR activities undertaken by it during each financial year in line with the requirements of Companies (Corporate Social Responsibility) Order, 2009. This may also include disclosure to the effect of compliance by companies with relevant industry/regulator guidelines or standards.

In addition to the SECP CSR guidelines, the National Accountability Bureau (NAB) has outlined an anti-corruption strategy, which includes corruption in the corporate sector. This strategy is of particular importance in the wake of a growing informal/black economy in Pakistan that represents enormous losses to the national exchequer. According to some estimates, Pakistan's informal/black economy is worth around Rs 9.3 trillion (US$9 billion), which is around 91.4 per cent of the total size of both official and unofficial GDP growth. The size of Pakistan's official economy is around Rs 3.5 trillion ($3 billion) – barely one third of the size of the informal economy (Rana 2013). Paying taxes and properly documentating transactions, therefore, are an important aspect of CSR in Pakistan. Corruption is, therefore, pervasive in Pakistan and, according to NAB, it is so entrenched in society that it has become a socially acceptable norm. Even those who are against corruption are often left with no alternative but to engage or collude in corrupt practices. The corporate sector in this regard is no exception.

In this connection, the National Accountability Bureau anti-corruption strategy is to deal with corruption in both public and private sectors. As already noted in Chapter 4, the genesis of corporate corruption in Pakistan was the absence of a business class following partition which resulted in state-sponsored top-down industrial development. The strong hold of state bureaucracy and a weak business class dependent on the state for corporate licenses (such as trade licenses) meant that businessmen's interaction with bureaucrats resulted in corrupt transactions, leading to the loss of revenue for the state and hardship for the corporate sector.

Moreover, NAB (2002) identifies corruption existing within the corporate sector and its dealings with society. Such corruption, according to NAB (2002: 66):

Has a massive impact on economic growth and development: it reduces investor and consumer confidence, degrades the spirit of competition, and compromises the quality and efficiency of outputs. Furthermore, private sector corruption has the potential to impact the individual in an acute way, via their savings and investments. The main victims are small to medium investors and consumers.

Some of the reasons for corruption in the corporate sector identified by NAB are the lack of professional standards and regulations, the corporate management culture, the lack of consumer protection and the lack of proper documentation of economy. The corporate sector suffers from weak professional standards and slipshod implementation of regulations (NAB 2002: 67). NAB reports that there is 'a large number of cases where chartered accountants were proven to have window dressed clients' accounts and, along with bankers, certified ownership of assets for the purposes of procuring loans and contracts' (NAB 2002: 67). In other cases, 'bank executives have been involved in major loan scams in return for a commission to turn a blind eye towards the viability of the project. Many of them are also involved in laundering money for their customers' (NAB 2002: 67).

Regarding consumer protection, there is hardly any consolidated law in Pakistan. Where sections in some other laws touch upon the role of consumer protection, they are significantly inadequate. Due to corrupt practices, the state regulators, instead of benefiting the consumers, use the piecemeal description of consumer protection in other laws to their own advantage (NAB 2002: 67).

Furthermore, as discussed in Chapter 4, with few exceptions corporations are managed by families. This has resulted in a failure to develop a modern professional corporate culture. Highly trained, experienced professional corporate managers, therefore, do not find openings in these organizations. Such a culture blocks the corporate sector's 'exposure to the international standards of business ethics and corporate governance, which emphasize the qualitative aspects of running a business' (NAB 2002: 67). Moreover, the lack of professionalism in corporate culture leads to undocumented economic transactions. With few exceptions, most businesses survive without keeping proper accounts. Not much is disclosed to official authorities, resulting in tax evasion and other malpractices (NAB 2002: 67). To deal with corporate-sector corruption the NAB (2002: 89) anti-corruption strategy proposes the following:

Formalization and documentation of the economy will increase the transparency of business activities. Secondly, we need to develop a sense of integrity within the professions, by institutional strengthening of their regulatory mechanisms, ethics management with a coalition of concerned professionals leading the way. Thirdly, consumers need better protection from abuse by the private sector. Consumer rights legislation and associations will be useful. Finally, the corporate sector must be encouraged to develop and enforce better standards of professional management and corporate governance.

Pakistan is known to have enough policies and strategies but not enough action. Since the introduction of the above anti-corruption strategy by NAB in 2002, nothing much has been achieved to properly document the economy and the black economy still thrives. Similarly, the corporate sector has hardly seen any improvement in professional standards and organizational culture. Documenting the economy still seems to be a major issue in Pakistan. The current minister for finance, Senator Muhammad Ishaq Dar, therefore, addressing the council members of the Institute of Chartered Accountants of Pakistan on Wednesday, 11 September 2013, said that documenting the economy, implementing good governance with a focus on transparency for public interest and revitalizing the economic structure of the country are the main priorities of the government (Imaduddin 2013). For this reason, the government has taken steps to utilize the expertise of chartered accountants and given them the position of 'Member' on various income tax tribunals. This provision was included in the Finance Bill 2013, which was passed by parliament and has now become part of the Finance Act, 2013[2] (Imaduddin 2013). If the government is able to achieve even the minimum in documenting the economy it will result in not only higher state revenues but also the documentation and professionalization of the corporate sector, inevitably creating more awareness within companies of the need to document their CSR activities as well.

Like SECP and NAB, the State Bank of Pakistan (SBP) has also introduced new regulatory frameworks for financial responsibility and probity (Waheed 2005: 27). In his keynote address at the 4th CEO Summit and book launch of *100 Business Leaders of Pakistan* at a hotel in Karachi on 8 November 2012, the governor of the SBP, Mr Yaseen Anwar, stressed the need for developing and implementing good governance practices in order to provide impetus for economic growth.

The SBP Prudential Regulations for Corporate/Commercial Banking Regulations require banks/development financial institutions (DFIs) to ensure that their business is conducted in conformity with high ethical standards and that banking laws and regulations are adhered to. The bank has also introduced strict relegations regarding money laundering (for details see SBP 2011: 31). Furthermore, according to these regulations, corporate/commercial banking and DFIs shall:

1. Strictly observe the following rules in the matter of making any donation/contribution for charitable, social, educational or public welfare purposes:
    ii) The total donations/contributions made by the bank/DFI during the year shall not exceed such amount as approved by their Board of Directors. It is expected that banks/DFIs making these

      donations/contributions would have already met provisioning and capital adequacy requirements.

    ii) The banks/DFIs shall develop policy/guidelines duly approved by the Board of Directors for making donations/contributions.

2. All donations or contributions to be made during the year must be specifically approved by the Board of Directors on pre or post facto basis as convenient.
3. Banks/DFIs are further directed to expressly disclose in their annual audited financial statements the total donation/contribution made during the year along with names of donees, to whom total donations/contributions during the year were made in excess of Rs 100,000. In the case of donations where any director or his family members have interest in the donee, the names of such directors, their interest in the donee and the names and addresses of all donees, shall also be given.

(SBP 2011: 27)

It is expected that the above regulations will improve corporate governance enhancing ethical business practices and accountability and might lead to the adoption of formal CSR policies by commercial banks and development finance institutions.

Conclusions

Generally, business corporations have considered CSR as a set of voluntary endeavours. However, in recent times, reflecting good governance trends and converging with the initiatives of international organizations like the UN Global Compact and the European Commission, governments have recognized that public administration and public policy initiatives have a key role in generating a better understanding of CSR. Governments, therefore, have started promoting CSR through soft law, quasi-voluntary standards and other incentives to move companies towards and beyond minimum regulatory goals. Government initiatives are also an outcome of challenges brought about by globalization and the changing economic environment leading to a changing role for business in society.

In this connection, several European countries, including Denmark, Finland, the Netherlands, Sweden, United Kingdom, Germany, Austria, Belgium and Luxembourg, have taken initiatives to promote CSR. Within the developing world, Indonesia, Malaysia and China are good examples of governments with a role in CSR. China particularly has become a leader among emerging markets. It has instituted new measures to promote CSR at various levels over the past decade. Some measures make use of existing institutions and incentive structures; others require legal compliance or regulatory mandates.

The Pakistani government has also recently taken the initiative to promote CSR. For example, as mentioned earlier, it has decided to set up the Pakistan Compliance Initiative Board to facilitate exporters, particularly small and medium enterprises, in meeting such international social compliance standards as ISO-9000, ISO-14000 and SA-8000. The basic intention is to take steps to encourage private companies to attain internationally recognized social compliance certification to stay in the world market.

In July 2013, the Security Exchange Commission of Pakistan also drafted corporate social responsibility guidelines. The basic objective of these guidelines is to promote the development of a framework for CSR initiatives by all companies. In addition to these guidelines for the corporate sector from the SECP, the National Accountability Bureau (NAB) has outlined its anti-corruption strategy, which includes corruption in the corporate sector. As part of its stategy, the NAB emphasizes the formalization and documentation of the economy. Companies are encouraged to carry out proper reporting and auditing of their accounts. The absence of this prevents companies from opting for written CSR polices and the reporting of CSR activities.

Moreover, the State Bank of Pakistan has also introduced new regulatory frameworks for financial responsibility and probity. It has introduced Prudential Regulations for Corporate/Commercial Banking. These regulations require banks/ development financial institutions (DFIs) to ensure that their business is conducted in conformity with high ethical standards and that banking laws and regulations are adhered to.

In conclusion, the above initiatives are a welcome sign. However, in the light of previous experience, where various governments have proved to be good at making plans, policies, legislation, etc., but have failed to deliver at the level of implementation, it has yet to be seen to what extent the government's initiatives to promote CSR in Pakistan will come to fruition.

Notes

1 For details see Albareda, Laura, Lozano, Josep M. & Ysa, Tamyko (2007) 'Public policies on corporate social responsibility: The role governments in Europe', *Journal of Business Ethics*, Vol. 74, No. 4, pp. 391–407.
2 The Finance Act, 2013 is a federal government finance bill applicable to the whole of Pakistan.

6 Perceptions and motivations of the indigenous corporate sector regarding CSR in Pakistan

This chapter analyses the perceptions of the indigenous corporate sector of CSR in Pakistan. In most cases, indigenous firms in Pakistan perceive CSR as corporate philanthropy with a mainly charitable purpose aimed at addressing the problems of disadvantaged, destitute and poor people. Ismail (2002) argues that though the terms philanthropy and charity are often used synonymously, they are different in meaning. Charity is used for the relief of an immediate need or a lack of something. Philanthropy, on the other hand, has a wider context – public benefit (Ismail 2002). Both involve giving for welfare purposes.

While some would view philanthropy as a Western construct, a rich tradition of philanthropy exists in the Islamic world, which has given rise to a range of educational, social and cultural institutions (Bremer 2004). Giving within Islam encompasses the concepts of both charity and philanthropy.

While all religions have encouraged both philanthropy and charity, it has only been codified in Islam (Baig & Ismail 2004). Islam identifies four different forms of charity i.e. *zakat, zakat-al-fitr, khairat* and *sadaqa*. *Zakat* is one of the five pillars on which the religion is built and the Qur'an (23: 1–4) says: *'Successful Indeed are the believers. Those who humble themselves in their prayers. Who avoid vain talk. Who are active in giving Zakat.'* *Zakat* is obligatory and more than a tax. It is a way to salvation for those who have accumulated wealth. According to Islam, when individuals fail to distribute *zakat*, it is the responsibility of the state to collect and distribute it (Baig & Ismail 2004). *Zakat-al-fitr* is a form of charity given to the poor after *Ramadan* – the holy month of fasting. *Khairat*, unlike *zakat*, is charity given voluntarily. *Sadaqa* is the voluntary giving of charity in expiation of sins or to ward off evil (Baig & Ismail 2004).

Ismail (2001) notes that, while *khairat* and *sadaqa* are charitable in nature since they meet the immediate needs of the poor, *zakat* is philanthropic (Ismail 2001). With reference to *zakat*, Ismail (2001: 1) states:

> It is meant to be used to empower the recipient such that (s) he is able to earn a livelihood, and is, thereafter, not listed among the needy. This would make the recipient a productive member of society, thereby contributing to the larger public well-being.

Since the corporate sector perceives CSR as corporate philanthropy and charity in Pakistan due to the religious orientation and long traditions of philanthropy and charity on the Indian subcontinent, it is important to discuss the role of both in CSR in Pakistan.

To begin with, it is pertinent to ask whether religion has any role to play in strengthening CSR. Brammer *et al.* (2007) have made a case for the role of religion in CSR and have forcefully argued that all organized religions provide definite guidelines for firms to practice CSR:

> Organized religion has sought to play a significant role in establishing and disseminating moral and ethical prescriptions that are consistent with religious doctrines and that offer practical guidance to those involved in business concerning ethical conduct. For example, the interfaith declaration on business ethics was developed to codify "the shared moral, ethical and spiritual values" of Christianity, Islam and Judaism in order to "draw up a number of principles that might serve as guidelines for international business behavior" (Interfaith Declaration, 1993: 2).
>
> (Brammer *et al.* 2007: 229)

Being a multifaceted concept, CSR refers to 'employee relations, community relations, issues concerned with women and minorities, environmental responsibility and product safety' (see Griffin & Mahon 1997; Hillman & Keim, 2001; Johnson & Greening 1999, as cited in Brammer *et al.* 2007: 232). Different religions have addressed these issues. For example, Judaism has identified the following as relevant to CSR: the philosophy of *caveat emptor* is unacceptable regarding the quality of products and pricing; the producer is required to identify material defects to consumers; weapons can only be sold to the state government to protect its citizens and protection against activities not permitted by the law of the land and not to those who would use them for illegal purposes (Brammer *et al.* 2007: 232).

Furthermore, poverty alleviation is of particular importance in Judaism, which engenders a deep appreciation of poverty and the needs of the poor and advocates assisting the poor to meet absolute needs such as food, housing, basic furniture, etc., and relative needs measured in terms of a comparison with the individual's previous standard of living (Brammer *et al.* 2007: 232).

Similarly in Islam, protection of health and life is supreme, and it 'goes further than Judaism by prohibiting Muslims from the sale of some products or services (like cigarettes, alcohol and gambling) that have been legalized by society but still cause considerable harm' (Brammer *et al.* 2007: 232).

Regarding the environment, some indirect prescriptions are also evident (Brammer *et al.* 2007). For example, 'in Islam, God is the creator and owner of wealth and material possessions, and Muslims are viewed as trustees of the earth on behalf of God' (Qur'an, 20: 6, as cited in Brammer *et al.* 2007: 232–33). Islam prohibits any destruction of nature created by God and advocates the protection of everyone's well-being when disposing of resources (Brammer *et al.* 2007: 232). Regarding other religions, Brammer *et al.* (2007: 233) note that:

> Among major faiths, the natural environment is perhaps viewed as having the greatest significance within Buddhism. This stems from the recognition of mutual interdependence of all things and the desire to avoid doing harm to any living thing (Brown 2000; Daniels 2003; Inoue 1997). Jews believe that mankind does not own nature, 'the earth is the Lord's and the fullness thereof', and, as in Islam, Jews are trustees for God and are duty bound to respect the integrity of nature.

Furthermore, according to Brammer *et al.* (2007: 232), Catholicism has long been supportive of workers' rights and promoted the concept of protecting the dignity of employees. The encouragement of fair labour practices is explicit in Islam too (Brammer *et al.* 2007: 232). Overall, all religions advocate social justice, which if absent causes human beings to be humiliated and is thus not endorsed by God, and in the case of Pakistan, Islamic religion has specifically provided the basis for charitable giving. Nevertheless, the Islamic tradition on the Indian subcontinent has been influenced by other religious traditions as well.

A long history of philanthropic activities in Pakistan has also contributed to the trend of philanthropy in general as well as to corporate philanthropy. The history of philanthropy in the part of the Indian subcontinent that became Pakistan goes back 5,000 years (Seljuq 2005). Together with the teachings and practices of Hinduism, Buddhism, Islam, Christianity and Sikhism, the roots of indigenous philanthropy are in a joint family system, professional guilds and centuries-old community living (Seljuq 2005).

Buddhist stupas, Hindu monasteries, Muslim *khanqahs* (Sufi monasteries) and Sikh *Gurdwaras* were the centre of philanthropic/charitable activities. In Pakistan, the shrine of Data Ganj Bakhsh[1] has offered free meals to the poor for a thousand years (Seljuq 2005). Similarly, in Islamkot (in Sindh province, 'a resting place is provided to the cattle and beasts of burden by the Bhagat Nano Ram Ashram, a facility not to be found anywhere else in the region'(Seljuq 2005: 85).

Hindu temples and ashrams were centres of community services for the sick, the poor and disadvantaged people – a tradition that continues today. Welfare activities focused on the poor and the sick; the concern for education was limited, being restricted to Hindu clerics who were Brahmans – the highest caste in Hinduism (Seljuq 2005: 85). In 250 BC, Buddhism started to grow within the geographical boundaries of what is now Pakistan. Buddhism was against the caste system and advocated welfare based on the principles of generosity, benevolence, cooperation and services to humanity through philanthropy and charity (Seljuq 2005: 85). Buddhists established a network of monasteries for social welfare as well as poverty alleviation purposes. Since they were against the caste system, they established religious universities for all. Traders also looked after community welfare. They 'performed in a wide spectrum ranging from fixation of market rates, wages, arrangements of loans and other allied professional obligations to purely social matters like marriage, death, widows, orphans and also all other issues faces by their members' (Seljuq 2005: 87). It is well known that traders were the vanguard progressive force behind Buddhist reforms on the Indian subcontinent, and were very active in corporate philanthropy at that time. Buddhist philanthropy, therefore, laid down the foundations of equality free of caste discrimination.

In 711 AD, Muhammad Bin Qasim conquered India and introduced Islam to the Indus valley. This initiated a new chapter of philanthropy and charity as prescribed in the Islamic religion. He introduced welfare programmes, established new religious schools and even granted a subsidy of 3 per cent of government revenues to the Brahmans to sustain the charitable work carried out by Hindu temples (Seljuq 2005). In a later period, probably around 1000–28, religious figures and Sufis migrated to the Indus valley and initiated missionary activities in an organized manner.

In 1469, Guru Nanak preached what became Sikhism and began another chapter of social welfare activity on the Indian subcontinent. The focus of Sikhism was on health care, education and providing relief to the poor. Sikh *gurdwaras* became sites of welfare activities, helping the destitute and needy. Sikh pantheistic doctrines such as *'I am you and you are me'* have played a considerable role in the expansion of community service over the centuries (Seljuq 2005).

During the British colonial period, the government introduced modern social welfare activities and established several institutions in the education and health sectors along modern Western lines. It was in the interest of the British government to involve the private sector and private non-profit sectors and share the responsibility of community development. It helped the British government develop closer relations with local people. The idea was to stabilize colonial rule.

Private individuals were therefore encouraged by the colonial government to start social institutions, with the Societies Registration Act of 1860 providing a legal basis (Bonbright & Azfar 2000). Diverse individuals and communities in the region were prompted to establish a myriad of social institutions to address welfare, health, education, shelter and cultural concerns. Some notable institutions are still active in Pakistan, including the Dyal Sing Majithia Trust (1895), Anjuman-e-Himayat-e-Islam (1886) and Nadirshaw Edulji Dinshaw College, which is now a leading engineering university (Bonbright & Azfar 2000). The trust that sustained this college also helped construct the Lady Dufferin Hospital in Karachi, which, with the joint efforts of the government and local philanthropists, started providing medical care to women across northern India (Bonbright & Azfar 2000).

The best-known Indian philanthropist of the colonial period is Sir Ganga Ram, who was given his knighthood in recognition of his services. Through the Ganga Ram Trust he created:

the Sir Ganga Ram Free Hospital, Hailey College of Commerce, Lady Maclagan Girls' High School, Ravi Road House of the Disabled, Hindu and Sikh Widows Home, Hindu Students Career Society, Home and School for Hindu and Sikh Widows, and the Lady Maynard Industrial School for Sikh and Hindu Women and Girls. His educational and health care charities were open to all, while the institutions for widows were exclusively for Hindus and Sikhs who suffered from widow customs not prevalent amongst Muslims.

(Bonbright & Azfar 2000: 14)

Although the philanthropic tradition is informed by a number of religions – including Islam on the Indian subcontinent and also religions from elsewhere – and provides references to human welfare that touch upon certain ethical aspects of CSR, no religion provides a comprehensive theory of CSR in terms of its quintessential relationship with economic growth and human development – a concept different from mere human welfare. The distinction between development and welfare can be defined thus: welfare deals with the consequences of the inequality and injustice that cause human suffering, and development deals with both the consequences and the causes of human suffering (Malik 2001). The concept of development is, therefore, political. Nevertheless, it is also well known that development work includes welfare projects in sectors such as health and education. Theoretically, what makes development political are the rights-based approaches to development, participation, capacity building and empowerment and issues of state governance.

Overall, it can be said that further evolution of CSR in Pakistan cannot be expected to be of a Western type. As will be shown in the latter part of this chapter, the current perceptions of CSR in Pakistan are deeply rooted in the country's historical traditions of philanthropy and charitable work and will probably evolve further as a result of the same historical heritage.

Perceptions of CSR

For reasons described above, perceptions of CSR within the local corporate sector do not go beyond philanthropic/charitable work. As shown in Figure 6.1, 38 per cent of organizations define CSR as 'employees' welfare', 48.4 per cent as 'welfare of the community'[2] and 13.6 per cent as 'paying taxes'.

Employees' welfare

When asked about their company's definition of corporate social responsibility, 38 per cent of companies defined CSR as something pertaining to employees' welfare. Employees' welfare included: good salaries/benefits, good working environment, opportunities to grow, self-respect, social security and sharing employees' problems whether monetary or non-monetary in times of need. Many companies gave examples of how they have helped their employees in the past. The following views of CEOs and other senior officials are instructive for understanding the perceptions companies have of CSR:

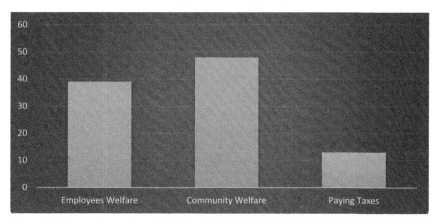

Figure 6.1 Perceptions about CSR

By law we do not have any obligation but being a company sensitive to its social responsibility, we always try to build a better environment within the company through employees' welfare. We believe charity begins from home and we consider our employees as part of the family. If family members or close relatives need assistance in difficult times, we feel it is our religious obligation to fulfill such needs.

The foremost social responsibility we have is to fulfill the social and economic needs of our employees. We initiate a number of projects to support a number of employees who are economically poor. Moreover, we initiate a number of programs for those who work for us on a project-to-project basis. When the project finishes their contracts are also concluded. The welfare of such employees is a top priority for us. If God has given us wealth, it is our foremost responsibility to fulfill the needs of people close to us.

It is our social responsibility to fulfill the needs of our employees. If our employees are not able to fulfill their needs such as educational needs of their children, girls' marriages, health requirements, we design programs to assist them with fulfilling such needs. In addition, if after fulfilling employees' needs we are left with some surplus resources, only then we think of contributing something towards the general welfare of the society. We consider our employees as part of our *biradari* (extended family)

Employees' welfare, community development and paying taxes, all are important aspects of social responsibility and it becomes difficult at times to make priority while giving resources. However, we give first priority to the people close to us, i.e. our employees.

Our company's policy is to support our employees in difficult times. Although we pay medical allowances to our employees but even then if someone has to bear a medical expense beyond his reach or someone's wife or children need some medical treatment that he cannot afford then we pay all the bills for that person. Apart from medical treatment, we support our employees if they have a genuine need that they cannot afford to fulfill.

Employee's welfare is our top priority as they feed so many families and their welfare means the welfare of so many people. Islam emphasizes caring about those close to you.

Employees' welfare is important. We have a policy of social security for our employees, which is compulsory. Moreover, we provide employees old age benefits. If someone gets ill, no matter how much the medical cost incurred for his/her recovery, it is the responsibility of the social security department to pay the bills.

It is an acknowledged fact all over the world that unless you have a skilled and satisfied workforce, you cannot bring success to your business. Therefore, it is our foremost priority to do whatever is required to make our employees satisfied at all levels.

We do not allow child labour. We have skilled labour whom we provide residence in which all utilities are free. Moreover, we take care of them regarding health and all other needs. This is our gift to God.

The above views have religious connotations in terms of employees' welfare, but at the same time, though not in contradiction of religious beliefs, they reflect a certain indigenous management culture. As explained in Chapter 2, this culture is embedded in the deinstitutionalized work environment created by family-dominated business structures. Pakistani society is still largely kinship-orientated. That kinship is of critical importance in Pakistan is something on which all the academics agree. In a culture dominated by kinship values even in the corporate sector, employees are considered part of the extended family and the notion that 'charity begins at home' allows corporate leaders to fulfill religious obligations too.

Community welfare

The second category after employees' welfare was the welfare of communities (in nearby areas or anywhere in the country): 48.4 per cent of companies defined CSR as community development. Their concept of community development ranged from providing monetary and non-monetary support on a one-time as well as an annual basis to initiatives such as: service delivery (health, education, sanitation and helping the disabled), human rights, women's rights, children's rights, etc.

Paying taxes

Another important aspect defined as CSR was paying taxes. In the view of some companies, paying taxes was the most important characteristic of good citizenship and a socially responsible corporate organization: 13.8 per cent of organizations upheld this view. They opined that every company should fulfill such an obligation. CEOs who considered paying taxes as the most important aspect of CSR had the following views:

> We give donations to various institutions from time to time and partici-pate in social development activities, but our first priority is to pay taxes so that the government can use them for people's welfare.
>
> I think it is very essential that each business pay taxes in the first place. Those who do not pay taxes are not fulfilling their social responsibility. The top priority regarding corporate social responsibility therefore is to pay taxes. Without paying taxes, there cannot be any progress on a larger scale in the country as these taxes are spent on people's welfare. The government will not be able to provide any services unless we pay taxes. The second priority after paying taxes is employee's welfare, as no man-agement can survive unless its employees are satisfied with their jobs. Then in the end if a company has enough resources it should invest in community development in the neighborhood and later at any place throughout the country.
>
> It is obvious that paying taxes is everyone's foremost responsibility and we have a clear-cut policy towards paying all taxes levied on us. We believe that if our country is giving us so much we must give back what we owe to the country.
>
> We should pay taxes as the government is poor and those who have resources are very rich.
>
> Giving taxes is the top social responsibility as taxes are the only source of the government's income. Without taxes, no government can run its business.

While emphasizing the importance of paying taxes as an essential aspect of corporate social responsibility, many organizations emphasized that the corporate sector, apart from paying taxes, is also contributing to society through its com-mercial activities. For example, they mentioned that it is providing millions of jobs, goods and services to society. Since the revenue department is notorious for corruption, tax evasion in Pakistan is common. Paying taxes, therefore, was considered important to enable the state to contribute to people's welfare.

Motivations behind CSR

The dominant motivation behind corporate giving is religious and religious-cum-social awareness rooted in the historical traditions of indigenous philanthropy/charity and community living. The spirit behind social motivation is, however, religious too, i.e. to fulfill the religious obligation of *huquq-ul-ibad* (individuals' rights). The dominant trend was therefore not human development in the modern sense. However, a small percentage of companies identified a business case for corporate giving, i.e. wealth creation and economic growth and distribution.

Table 6.1 Motivations behind corporate giving

Reasons	Percentage
Charity for religious reasons	50.90
Charity for religious-cum-social reasons	33.10
Because corporate giving is linked with wealth creation and overall economic growth	16.00
Total	100

According to the survey, 50.9 per cent of companies were motivated to make social contributions for religious reasons, and 33.1 per cent thought it was their religious as well as social responsibility (as ascribed in religion). However, 16 per cent of companies considered that they were contributing to overall economic growth and wealth creation. See Table 6.1.

Charity for religious reasons

As described above, the main motivation behind corporate giving was meeting religious obligations through philanthropic and charitable work. CEOs had two different definitions of such work, the dominant one being helping the poor by giving money, food or any other thing on a one-off basis, and the other being supporting people on a long-term basis so that they are able to work and stand on their feet and not require charity again. Some common views of CEOs are instructive in understanding companies' perceptions in this area:

> Our prophet said, 'Propitiatory offerings *(sadaqa)* relieve you of troubles/evils. The unseen problems turning on you go away. What other reason there can be behind giving charity.'
>
> Faith is incomplete without giving charity. If it becomes a social practice and everybody starts giving charity, the social responsibility of individuals as well as the business sector will be fulfilled.
>
> Since those on whom God has bestowed worldly delights/privileges and those who are deprived of these are to be judged by God, those who are privileged must think how they have used the privileges of life as they have greater responsibility towards society and will be judged on that.
>
> The Shariah enforces charity *(zakat)*. In my opinion, those who do not give *zakat* should be excluded from Islam. *Zakat* purifies one's riches.

Religious as well as social motivation behind philanthropic/charity work

There were a number of CEOs who did philanthropic/charity work for not only religious but also social reasons. The electronic and print media, which have introduced several programmes on social issues in Pakistan, appear to have contributed significantly to social awareness within the corporate sector. The following views of CEOs and other senior officials reflect religious-cum-social thinking around philanthropic/charity work:

> I certainly believe that it is our moral and social duty to return something back to society, which brought fortune for us, mainly to serve humanity and the economic wellbeing of everyone within society. The basic principle of a good society is growth accompanied by equality. We see sites of poverty and inequality resulting in growing crime and a deteriorating law and order situation on television every day. The private and public sectors together should do more about society.

> We provide charity on a one-off basis every year, but importantly, we support individuals by providing loans to start some business/work and once they are established they are required to give the loans back. We also provide our own manufactured soap to deserving individuals so that they can sell them and earn money for themselves. This is how they become independent in the end and do not require our support in the long run.

> According to our religious faith if God has given you enough resources, you should distribute them to others. Moreover, there is a social dimension behind charity. How is it possible that you can live in peace when others around you are in misery? It is appalling to see misery all around reported by media.

> We have gone through all the stages in our struggle to become a big business company and therefore we have a full recognition of social problems and our own social responsibilities. We are living in this society and our own betterment is linked with the overall progress of the society.

> There can be no second opinion about the fact that society and we are part of each other. Whether we acknowledge it or not we do owe a lot to society. Religion is also important and can play an important role.

> We owe a lot to society. If we were living in the jungle only then we could afford to ignore our social responsibility and society's needs. Since we are living in society, our own growth is very much linked with overall societal growth.

Wealth creation/economic growth

For this category, companies were asked whether corporate social responsibility has anything to do with wealth creation and overall economic growth in society. A great number of companies (mainly medium and small, but also some large companies) did not have a clear idea of how CSR can contribute to economic growth and wealth creation in society through development. They opined that their commercial activities were already creating wealth and contributing to economic growth. That corporate sector contributions in the form of social investment can help create new wealth and contribute to economic growth was a largely dormant concept. However, when the concept was defined in its full sense, some companies responded positively and emphasized that there needed to be more awareness of this aspect of CSR within the corporate sector in Pakistan. Nevertheless, there were some companies with a clear vision of CSR in terms of economic growth, wealth creation and distribution. Moreover, those who defined CSR as paying taxes emphasized the documentation of the economy as an essential aspect of economic growth and distribution and argued that paying taxes is an essential aspect of CSR that serves the same ends.

Those CEOs and other senior officials who had an understanding of CSR's role in economic growth and wealth creation and distribution opined that:

> CSR is important for creating new wealth and overall economic growth. The main reason is that if we do not invest in people, they will not be able to buy things and there will be no economic growth.
>
> It is obvious that the corporate sector is part of society. If there will be overall development in society and people in society become prosperous, they will perform better and there will be growth in industry boosting the economy as well.
>
> We are in the field of consultancy and want to have a developed society through the eradication of poverty. Poverty alleviation can help the poor be more productive and contribute to the overall economic growth of society.
>
> Economic growth is linked to the documentation of the economy, therefore, we make sure that we pay taxes. I think if everyone pays taxes, they can significantly contribute to economic growth and wealth creation.

Conclusions

Due to a long tradition of philanthropic and charitable work by people belonging to different religions, particularly Islam, within the geographical boundaries that became Pakistan in 1947, the dominant motivation behind CSR within the indigenous corporate sector was religious. For this reason, therefore, most companies defined CSR as community welfare, second to which was employees' welfare. In a joint family-based society, employees' welfare was also considered as supporting the wider public cause. This is because individuals support their families (in some cases even their brothers, sisters and cousins) and when it comes to philanthropic/charity work they are counted as families, not as individuals. Supporting employees, therefore, means supporting individuals in their families.

The sense of being gifted by God and a profound belief in the omnipotence of God, together with a concern for the health and happiness of their employees – and community members – has, however, given birth to a religious-cum-social motivation behind social contributions. This social awareness is further strengthened by several areas of misery in society, which corporate leaders witness themselves and that keep hammering at their moral conscience through the print and electronic media.

Though not many in number, it is interesting to note that some companies defined their motivation behind CSR purely in economic terms. In their view, CSR helps generate new wealth and distribution. The documentation of the economy and the payment of taxes was also considered important in this connection.

Overall, however, a religious motivation behind CSR for community and employee welfare was dominant. It has been demonstrated in this chapter that religion does have a role in CSR, as the concerns of CSR in terms of human well-being, poverty, human rights, the environment, etc., are addressed by various religions. The main difference between religious beliefs and modern CSR, however, is that religion deals with the above issues in moral and ethical terms, whereas modern CSR is rooted in modern theories of commerce, economics, law and political science. What is probably required in developing countries such as Pakistan is to transform the religious-cum-moral understanding of CSR into a modern one, instead of superimposing a Western type of CSR from the very outset.

Notes

1 Data Ganj Bakhsh was a Persian Sufi scholar, writer and poet who lived in the fifth century AH (eleventh century AD).
2 The respondents included human rights as part of community welfare.

7 CSR policies and practices

This chapter is an attempt to analyze the sensitivity of corporate social responsibility measured through the CSR policies (written as well as unwritten) and practices of small, medium and large corporate organizations in Pakistan.

Current studies based on secondary data (such as: Naeem & Welford 2009; Nazir 2009) have either attempted to analyze the written policies regarding human rights, the environment and anti-corruption measures of corporate organizations operating in Pakistan (see Naeem & Welford 2009) or have studied the corporate environmental governance issues and practices of Pakistani firms (see Nazir 2009). It is important to note that in a developing country such as Pakistan, not all local companies that make resources available for welfare or development have policies and, of those that follow some policy, only a few have articulated written policies – others follow unwritten policies. An analysis only of those companies that have written policies is inadequate to portray the overall picture of the nature of CSR in Pakistan. Our survey, therefore, collected data relating to written as well as unwritten CSR policies and companies that donate but have no policy at all.

Corporate social responsibility (CSR) policies

According to the survey, 27.2 per cent of companies had a CSR policy compared to the large segment of companies – 72.8 per cent – that did not have a CSR policy. See Table 7.1.

Among those with some kind of CSR policy, 63.4 per cent of companies had a written policy and 36.6 per cent had an unwritten policy. See Table 7.2.

'Written policies' refer to companies (mainly large national) that have a strategic understanding of and vision regarding their social role and contribution. 'Unwritten policies' refer to those companies that make resources (both monetary and non-monetary) available for welfare or development on a yearly basis. Such policies are usually based on CEO or family priorities, are mainly philanthropic/charitable in nature and generally lack a strategic vision regarding CSR. Unwritten policies also refer to informal guidelines developed for a particular year regarding the corporate contribution to charitable causes,

Table 7.1 Percentage of companies with a CSR policy

Policy?	No.	Percentage
Yes	41	27.2
No	110	72.8
Total	151	100

Table 7.2 Percentage of companies with written and unwritten CSR policies

If 'Yes'	No.	Percentage
Written	26	63.4
Unwritten	15	36.6
Total	41	100

Table 7.3 Reasons for companies having no CSR policy

Response	Percentage
Lack of awareness	20.40
Lack of interest	32.30
Lack of resources	21.10
Nobody had approached them and therefore never thought of it	10.40
New company	15.80
Total	100

or are demand-based, i.e. corporate support is provided to individuals, NGOs, employees and community members only if they ask for it. Together, these two types of policies provide an overall policy profile of CSR in Pakistan.

Reasons for companies not having a written or unwritten policy

As shown in Table 7.3, 20.4 per cent of companies identified lack of awareness regarding social contributions as the main factor for their not having a CSR policy. The percentage that identified lack of interest as the reason for not having a written or unwritten CSR policy was the highest; 32.2 per cent of companies upheld this view. Lack of resources was considered to be the main factor for not having a policy by 21.1 per cent of organizations, and 10.4 per cent of companies informed us that it was because no one (e.g. neither trusts nor NGOs) had ever approached them for systematic or organized support and therefore they did not think of having such a policy. About 15.8 per cent of companies suggested that new companies usually do not have a corporate social policy.

Based on the semi-structured interviews, further analysis of the reasons for companies lacking a CSR policy is in order.

Lack of awareness

Companies do not have a good idea of CSR in Pakistan. In a general way, CEOs or their families do a considerable amount of philanthropic/charitable work on an individual basis; however, unlike what might be the case in industrially advanced countries, companies in Pakistan do not have much awareness of the importance of CSR for development and economic growth. On the whole there is no organized CSR movement in Pakistan. It is mainly individuals such as CEOs who determine companies' decisions about social investment. For obvious reasons, therefore, there is a lack of organized systems for corporate investment aimed at development. As a CEO remarked in this context:

> Western societies have evolved very definite systems for social investment. They plan and channel their resources in a very systematic way and that is why they get better results. This surely is possible through written CSR policies and we need to create such awareness in Pakistan. Institutions such as Chambers of Commerce in Pakistan need to design programs for the awareness of companies about the causes of development problems in the society and the need to work for sustainable development, instead of one-time philanthropic giving. Also, they need to be made aware of the benefits they can get through an organized CSR activity guided by a written CSR policy.

Some other views by CEOs are also instructive:

> One reason is that people do not have resources and the other is that people have no awareness about the benefits they will get from their organized development work.
>
> Generally, there is a lack of awareness. People are not aware of the benefits of formulating written CSR policies for companies as well as their stakeholders.
>
> Pakistan is an under-developed country and people having considerable resources and spending a lot of money for the general welfare of communities are not aware of the importance and benefits of having a definite corporate social policy.

Some CEOs were of the view that civil society organizations in advanced industrial societies have played an important role in creating awareness in society and in the corporate sector. Such a role by civil society organizations in Pakistan has yet to be seen. The following views of CEOs in this connection are instructive:

> In the West, civil society organizations have played an important role in creating awareness of CSR and creating an environment of accountability for corporations. In Pakistan, civil society has yet to play this role and

make corporations aware of organized development activities by having written CSR policies. These organizations have neither created awareness, nor have created the environment of accountability making companies realize the importance of CSR.

People are not aware. Since corporate organizations are so busy doing their business operations, having some definite development policy has yet to be on their radar. NGOs need to create such awareness.

Lack of awareness is the basic cause for not having definite policies for the welfare of society. The main reason is that no one has ever approached companies and has not made them realize about the importance of having written policies for development. I believe if welfare/development organizations approach companies and make them aware of the benefits of written development policies, most big companies possessing a huge amount of resources will probably adopt written CSR policies.

Many companies do not even know what written development policy means and what its importance is for the betterment of society. Once they are informed about this, they would surely like to have one. We must have some sort of NGOs or NGO networks that could create awareness on this issue.

Social welfare organizations/NGOs have not created such an environment in which companies could get awareness about the importance of having definite corporate social policy. If such an environment is created, many companies will consider having such a policy.

Other reasons

Other reasons identified by companies were: lack of interest, lack of resources, no welfare or development organization having ever approached them in relation to organized CSR activities, and being a new company. Small and medium-sized companies usually lack substantial profits and resources and are not in a position to plan long-term CSR programmes or formulate written policies for such programmes. Though several medium-sized companies did have some kind of formal (albeit unwritten) policy, they were constrained by a lack of surplus resources for long-term planning regarding CSR. These companies, therefore, did not have a written policy, articulating their policies and taking decisions in the light of the resources available in a particular year. Small companies do not have sufficient resources to systematically commit to giving something back to society. They can contribute on a one-off basis and usually if someone approaches them.

Some senior management individuals commented on companies' lack of interest as the main reason for not having a CSR policy. This, they thought, is true for companies that only engage in one-off charity work usually peripheral to the main business – always the first thing to go when the push comes to shove. A comment by a senior manager in a large national company is instructive:

Everyone has awareness about the importance of social work. The main reason for not having a definite policy for such work is selfishness and lack of interest [and] Even those having a lot of resources don't consider it important to have a definite corporate policy for sustainable development. It is because most people are self-centered. They are more concerned about their own growth and not that of the society they are living in.

Another important reason found for the lack of interest and motivation with regard to formal policy is religion. This is because making a social contribution is mainly conceived of as a form of charity. Charity, as preached by the Islamic religion, is a way of bringing justice to society. Moreover, justice is the essence of religion. Islam has therefore made charity (that is, *Zakat*) obligatory and binding upon all those who embrace the faith. The main motivation is the possibility of spiritual reward. The rule is that 2.5 per cent of a wealthy Muslim's savings must be donated to the poor. Publicizing or showing off is socially considered un-Islamic and for this reason most companies providing charity prefer that others do not know about it. A religious saying is often quoted: 'If you donate from one hand the other hand should not know about it.' Having a formal written policy in such a culture is not, therefore, desirable. It was also found that a few companies also provide resources to extremist religious activities in the country. There are others who endeavour to turn their 'black' money into 'white' through charitable giving, which prevents them having any ongoing formal written CSR policy.

Who makes the decisions about corporate giving?

As discussed in Chapter four, Pakistan's corporate sector is weak, 'dependent on state patronage, and prone to structural deficiencies' (Ali & Malik 2009: 29). The manufacturing sector has a narrow base and investment in this sector has more or less stagnated in the past few decades (Ali & Malik 2009: 29). Ongoing political instability and poor public infrastructure have slowed industrial growth. As a result, Pakistan's industrial sector has failed to achieve growth and reduce poverty on a sustainable basis. Corporate management revolves around the individuals or families that own the business and is unprepared to meet the challenges brought about by globalization. The culture of family-based businesses becomes a disincentive for decentralized, institutionalized management systems. Approximately 80 per cent of employment is generated by family businesses in Pakistan (Afghan & Wiqar 2007). Such businesses are based on a succession of leadership within a family, i.e. once the father retires, his children take over. Citing several scholars, Afghan and Wiqar note that:

> Succession is viewed by many scholars as a long-term process involving multiple activities (Handler 1994; Sharma, Chrisman & Chua 2003). Longenecker and Schoen (1978), for instance, have pointed out that a

successor's training takes place throughout childhood, adolescence and adult years. Their basic propositions is as follows: 'child succession in the leadership of a family-controlled business involves a long-term diachronic process of socializations, that is, family successors are gradually prepared for leadership through a lifetime of learning experience (Longenecker and Schoen, 1978: 1).

(Afghan & Wiqar 2007: 1–2)

Family-based business is a result of the strong *biradari* system. *Biradari* may be understood as patrilineal kinship (Lyon 2004). In Pakistan, it is a social category; it is not ideologically or religiously constructed and, though related, is not synonymous with caste as is the case in Hinduism (Alvi 2001: 53). Geographically, members of a *biradari* live in many parts of the country. It is through the *biradari* system that patronage is maintained in both business and politics. In business, the *biradari* system is privileged to ensure the loyalty of family or extended family members to the business. In the hiring of key staff, merit is secondary (Afghan & Wiqar 2007).

Hiring members of the *biradari* and maintaining the *biradari* network is also instrumental in gaining the support and patronage of the state bureaucracy. There are historical reasons for this. Unlike industrially advanced countries, including India, the industrialization process in Pakistan was not initiated directly by the bourgeois class. This class was weak, lacking any roots in the areas that now constitute Pakistan and not fully developed at the time of the inception of the country. Thus, the industrialization process did not evolve from within society but was introduced by the state from above. Money for the same was often channeled through bureaucrats, and their discretionary judgments became an effective factor in policymaking. State-sponsored industrial development provided opportunities for bureaucrats to establish industry as well and gave birth to a centralized management culture that revolved around individuals and their families.

It is not surprising, therefore, that according to our survey, in 98 per cent of companies CEOs make the decisions about corporate giving (see Table 7.4). A CEO stated in this connection:

> Since I take all major decisions about the business, I think it becomes important that I should be taking all decisions about investing in the social sector as well. However, once decisions are made then human resource people and people from some other departments implement the decisions.

There were only 2 per cent of companies in which decision-making was relatively decentralized and finance directors or directors of administration or other senior officials were found to be taking decisions about corporate giving.

An interesting correlation was found between companies' decision-making policies and their CSR policies. As shown in Table 7.5, of the 27.2 percent of

Table 7.4 People responsible for decisions about corporate giving

	No.	Percentage
Chief Executive Officer	148	98
Finance Director	2	1.3
Human Resource Director/Manager	1	0.7
Total	151	100

Table 7.5 Correlation between decision-making policies and CSR policies

Decision-maker for CSR policymaking	CSR policy		No CSR policy		Written		Unwritten	
	No.	%	No.	%	No.	%	No.	%
CEO	39	95	109	99	24	61.53	15	38.47
CEO's family	0	0	0	0	0	0	0	0
Finance Manager	2	5	0	0	2	8	0	0
HR Director/ Manager	0	0	1	1	0	0	0	0
Senior management	0	0	0	0	0	0	0	0
Total	41	100	110	100	26	100	15	100

companies (frequency 41) with a policy, CEOs were responsible for devising CSR policy in 95 per cent (frequency 39) and finance managers had that responsibility in only 5 per cent. Where CEOs devised CSR policies, 61.53 per cent of the companies had written and 38.47 per cent had unwritten policies. This trend again shows the dominance of family-based business concerns in Pakistan, where in most cases CEOs make all company decisions, not just those pertaining to CSR policy.

Who implements the policies?

It was interesting to note that, in most cases – 90.7 per cent – the chief executive officer not only made all the decisions regarding CSR policy but implemented them too. After the CEO, in 9.3 per cent of companies a senior officer implemented companies' social policies. These officials head company departments such as finance, human resources (HR) and administration. In some companies, heads of two or more departments (for example, human resource and finance) were found to be implementing CSR policies. For details, see Table 7.6.

There was also a correlation between companies' CSR implementation policies and their CSR policies. As shown in Table 7.7, although in most cases CEOs implemented as well as devise company CSR policy, the implementation of policies was relatively decentralized. In 71 per cent of companies it was the CEO and in 7 per cent, 18 per cent, 2 per cent and 2 per cent of companies it was the finance managers, HR director/manager and other senior

Table 7.6 Who is responsible for the implementation of a company's policy?

Person	No.	Percentage
Chief Executive Officer	137	90.7
Other individual/individuals	14	9.3
Total	151	100

Table 7.7 The correlation between implementation policies and CSR policies

Decision-maker for CSR policymaking	CSR policy		No CSR policy		Written		Unwritten	
	No.	%	No.	%	No.	%	No.	%
CEO	29	71	108	98	17	58.63	12	41.37
CEO's family	3	7	1	1	3	12	0	0
Finance Manager	7	18	1	1	4	15	3	20
HR Director/ Manager	1	2	0	0	1	4	0	0
Senior management	1	2	0	0	1	4	0	0
Total	41	100	110	100	26	100	15	Total

official respectively who were found to be responsible for the implementation of CSR policies.

CSR activities

Companies support a variety of development and welfare projects in Pakistan. In most cases, the support is channeled directly to end beneficiaries. Other channels are NGOs or companies' own welfare organizations or trusts, etc. In terms of interest in supporting particular areas of development, companies' support areas ranged from health, education, environment, women's welfare and women's rights to human rights and children's rights, water supply, sanitation, income generation and micro-credit schemes.[1] With reference to the above-mentioned areas, organizations were asked to which areas they were currently channelling resources. Detail of their support in different areas is given below.

Health

As shown in Table 7.8, 45 or 29.8 per cent of companies were found to be currently supporting health. The areas within health that attracted support were family planning, hospitals/dispensaries, projects related to the rational use of drugs, and support for the Shaukat Khanum cancer hospital established by the famous cricketer-turned-politician, Imran Khan.

Table 7.8 Support for health

Health area	Responses	
	No.	*Percentage*
Family planning	1	2.20
Hospital/dispensary	36	80.00
Rational use of drugs	1	2.20

Table 7.9 Support for health by industrial sector

Industry	Family planning	Hospital/ dispensary	Rational use of drugs	Provide aid/ assistance to Shaukat Khanum	Free dispensary	Total
Leather	0	1	0	1	0	2
Food & Beverages	0	2	0	0	0	2
Trading	0	10	1	0	1	11
Auto Allied	0	1	0	0	1	2
Advertising/Print	0	0	0	0	1	1
Textiles	1	7	0	0	1	10
Sport	0	7	0	0	1	8
Services	0	0	0	0	1	1
Chemicals	0	2	0	0	0	2
Surgical	0	2	0	0	0	2
Electronics	0	1	0	0	0	1
Other	0	3	0	0	0	3
Total	1	36	1	1	6	45

Table 7.9 provides details of contributions to the health sector by industrial sector.

Considering the extremely poor health conditions in Pakistan, where the current ratios of population to health facilities are 1,127 persons per doctor, 14,406 per dentist and one hospital bed available for 1,786 persons (GoP 2013), it seems pertinent that 80 per cent of support goes to hospitals/dispensaries and 13.3 per cent to establishing free dispensaries.

Although adequate healthcare facilities have never been available, the privatization of the health sector has further excluded people from having their healthcare needs met. No changes to the insurance system or Band-Aid safety net can offset the negative impact of privatization on the great majority of ordinary people. Deficiencies in the public sector healthcare system are very serious – and the corporate sector is playing some role in mitigating these deficiencies.

The public sector healthcare system in Pakistan is a legacy of the colonial era, with arbitrary and awkward changes made after independence. It is fraught with anomalies, the overlapping of authority and responsibilities of different departments and an overall lack of vision. Most of these departments have been propped up by multilateral financial institutions to serve their own health agendas, which may or may not harmonize with local conditions and systems. These departments draw legitimacy from the funding they receive from donors and are not necessarily committed to their health objectives. This calls for an enhanced role for and collaboration between the indigenous corporate sector and civil society to pressure the government to formulate an integrated, comprehensive vision for health and align all efforts according to it. The new vision should define health as an individual and collective way of life and not simply as medicines, diagnostics and hospitals. It should include both civic quality of life and the environment on its agenda. Public health should not be considered as an isolated matter.

The above aspects of the healthcare system have to do with preventive healthcare that emphasizes health as a way of life. The dominant trend in Pakistan is to support a curative rather than preventive health system. In this connection, the comments of two CEOs are important:

> Health is a most important sector. There are many institutions that are running health centres but they are very expensive. In today's environmental conditions diseases are on the increase and a majority of people are suffering from various kinds of illnesses. Those who can afford medical expense are cured but a majority of the poor are deprived of getting any medical treatment. It becomes imperative therefore to support the poor in the health sector by hospital beds and dispensaries. It is our first priority therefore to support credible organizations supporting the poor in the health sector.
>
> Health is wealth but unfortunately the poor in this country are devoid of such wealth. We therefore support the Gulab Devi hospital on an annual basis to provide health facilities that the poor cannot afford.

Although none of the companies surveyed were currently supporting any projects in the area of health awareness, some companies nevertheless acknowledged their importance. A few CEOs, for example, laid stress on working for health awareness. They believed that 50 per cent of diseases could be cured simply by increasing the health awareness of people, especially those in the villages. Commenting on this, a CEO stated:

> It can be said in general that most people do not have awareness about health issues. There are a few seminars and news/articles on health issues in urban localities, but in rural areas there are no such programs that could make the villagers aware of their health issues. As a result, our rural population is completely ignorant about preventive aspects of health. In cities, there are some modern health facilities but in villages only unqualified quacks are providing medical treatment and since the literacy rate in villages is extremely low, they are completely ignorant about such illegal medical practices. It is most important therefore to

create health awareness in villages and we are willing to support such programmes in the health sector.

A few companies considered spending more on projects on the rational use of drugs in the future. In the view of a few CEOs, there are a number of diseases which require only inexpensive medicines and medical treatment, but commercialization in the health sector has made it difficult for ordinary people to behave rationally around medication. They therefore put emphasis on building advocacy campaigns related to the rational use of drugs. For example, a CEO commented: 'The most important issue within the health sector is the rational use of drugs. We intend to work on this issue and contribute significantly'.

Overall, the main motivation behind supporting the health sector was religious in nature. A number of CEOs emphasized the importance of the right to health being guided by Islam. According to them, it is a religious obligation to support those who are sick or weak due to illness and therefore not able to earn sufficiently to secure a decent life.

Education

Twenty per cent of companies extended their support to education. Of this 20 per cent, 60 per cent supported primary education, 16.7 per cent religious education, and 10 per cent gave cash awards to deserving students. In line with this, 6.7 per cent of support provided free education to deserving girls and boys at primary and secondary and 3.3 per cent of support was extended to one institution, the Citizen's Foundation, which is doing significant work for the provision of education for poor children. Details of the industry breakdown of current support in the education sector are given in Table 7.10.

After health and human rights, education was the priority area for support. According to the CEOs and other senior officials, only an educated society can progress. The spread of education not only enhances economic growth and benefits society overall, it also provides better-educated and skilled workers for the corporate sector. The saying, 'Knowledge is power', was often quoted by CEOs and they opined that the secret of development in industrialized countries was mass education; this needs to be achieved in Pakistan too.

Several CEOs' prioritization of contributions to the educational sector was guided by religious teaching, according to which knowledge leads to consciousness of God. For the Muslim, education is an obligation. A CEO commented: 'The Prophet said, "Seeking knowledge is an obligatory duty on all Muslims." This tradition clearly indicates that the education of young people, boys and girls, is a compulsory right to be fulfilled by their parents and the state.' Another CEO, while emphasizing the importance of education, cited prophet Muhammad's saying: 'What about some people who neither learn from their neighbors nor seek advice? By God if people do not teach their neighbours or learn from their neighbors, I will be quick in penalizing them.'

Table 7.10 Support for education by industrial sector

Industry	Primary education	Adult education	Only girls' primary education	Education of girls and boys at primary level	Preferably boys' education	Citizen foundation school	Religious education	Providing free education to boys and girls to intermediate stage	Help through award of cash prize	Total
Food & Beverages	1	0	1	0	0	0	0	1	0	3
Trading	3	1	0	1	0	1	3	1	2	10
Auto Allied	0	0	0	0	1	0	0	0	0	1
Advertising/ Print	0	0	0	0	0	0	1	0	0	1
Textiles	4	0	0	0	0	0	0	0	0	4
Sport	3	0	1	1	0	0	1	0	1	6
Surgical	2	0	0	0	0	0	0	0	0	2
Other	1	0	0	0	0	0	0	0	0	1
Total	14	1	2	2	1	1	5	2	3	28

Some CEOs also stressed that in Islam, learning is not limited to religious studies, but includes the study of all that may lead to the betterment of life. This, most of the CEOs seemed to be supportive of educational causes and many were already supporting educational projects, which included donating the entire school, supporting a number of poor children, running their own schools for poor children and providing scholarships to deserving students for vocational and IT training programmes. To illustrate how important the educational sector is for most of the CEOs interviewed, the following comments by them are instructive:

> Priorities have been confused in our society. Our national objectives are even not clear. People are also not aware of the importance of education advocated by Islam. In my personal opinion, unless we educate our nation no problems can be solved – the most important being economic. Unless people get gainful employment, economic development is not possible. Therefore providing education should be the top priority. When we review 66 years of Pakistan, we come to know that education has always been a least-priority area. As a result the literacy rate has remained dismally low.
> Basically education is linked with the concept of human resource development without which no other resource can be developed. Our priority therefore is always to invest in educational projects.

Some CEOs were more concerned about promoting IT training. A CEO, commenting on the importance of computer education, stated:

> It is a growing field the world over. In contemporary times becoming modern is inconceivable without developing a computer culture within society. My first priority therefore is to provide computer education and develop a community culture based on computer training. Moreover, the spread of computer culture can enable Pakistan to develop in software designing and so on and earn revenue for the country by marketing their products abroad.

The reason for education, and especially primary education, attracting the biggest share of corporate support is because education is one of the most neglected aspects of human development in Pakistan. According to the Pakistan Human Rights Report 2010, Pakistan's achievements in the education sector remained poor compared to other South Asian countries. In terms of the Human Development Index (HDI), the figure for expected years of schooling in Pakistan was only 6.8, while it was 10.3 in India, 8.1 in Bangladesh, 8.8 in Nepal and 12 in Sri Lanka (HRCP 2010: 254). In the Global Competitiveness Report 2010/2011, Pakistan was ranked 123 among 139 countries (HRCP 2010: 254). This ranking had fallen 22 places since 2009 due to low enrollment in primary, secondary and tertiary education (HRCP 2010: 254).

Despite the government's declaration of 2010/11 as the year of national literacy, in an effort to meet the educational targets set by the UN millennium development goals, there was once again no increase in the government's educational budget. This remained at a meagre 2 per cent of GDP for 2010/11 (HRCP 2010). Furthermore, compared to regional countries, Pakistan's allocation remained disappointing. For example, public sector expenditure on education was 3.2 per cent of GDP in Nepal, 3.3 per cent in India, and 5.2 per cent in Iran (HRCP 2010: 255).

More importantly, Rauf (1983) argues that the emphasis on education in Pakistan never went beyond a pseudo-scientific form of education. It did not promote real scientific thinking and scientific culture at a mass level. It only served to meet the manpower needs of labour-intensive food stuffs and primary goods required for the industrial production of countries in the First World. As for universal mass education, this has always been a low priority area (Rauf 1983: 336). In the eyes of state planners, no gains could be made from mass education. On the contrary, 'a socially conscious and literate population would like to see certain basic changes in the social sustructure, and would become a threatening prospect for those who prefer to maintain status quo' (Rauf 1983: 336). As a consequence of giving least importance to primary mass education in the early as well the later periods, there is a mass population of children who have become victims of child labour (Rauf 1983: 336) and many are recruited by *madrassahs* (religious schools) promoting religious extremism. Under the above circumstances, the corporate sector's support for primary education is the right response to the problems of literacy in Pakistan – though much more needs to be done.

Women's rights

Of a total population of 180 million, women comprise almost half. In other words, women make up at least 48.7 per cent of the population in Pakistan. It is therefore impossible to visualize any meaningful development or progress at national level without their optimum participation, but unfortunately this reality is far away. Women's social spaces are generally confined to stereotypical gender roles within the household.

Women face gender inequality in Pakistan, which puts them in a more vulnerable position than men. In the economic sphere, women face a lack of employment opportunities, inadequate pay and the violation of their rights in the workplace. They receive lower wages than men, even for the same work. For the last decade, most female workers have been concentrated in the informal sector of the economy, employed as domestic workers, and many unskilled women become sex workers. Women are more vulnerable to chronic poverty because of gender inequalities in the distribution of income, access to productive inputs such as credit, command over property and control over earned income, as well as gender bias in labour markets

Women's equal participation in economic and social development has also been hampered by certain social views and practices regarding gender issues and the division of labour between men and women. These can cover household matters such as women's domestic responsibilities, power relations between husbands and wives or public issues like women's access to decision-making. Traditional cultural views and stereotypical labels on women represent another source of risk. In many areas, women's inferior position has been worsened by violence and sexual abuse.

Women are denied equal excess to education and employment. Besides economic factors, women are not able to fulfill their social and psychological needs. They do not have a healthy life or social identity. Moreover, they face discriminatory laws such as the 'Hadood Ordinance', and such laws have become obstacles in the way of their social and economic participation in the nation-building process.

Women's empowerment and gender equality is considered a key to human development and is the third of the eight Millennium Development Goals. The indigenous corporate sector in Pakistan, however, seems to be less aware of the importance of women's rights for economic and social development. Women's rights, therefore, do not seem to be an important concern for indigenous companies in Pakistan. Only 3.3 of the companies surveyed actively supported women's rights issues. Moreover, the attitude of several CEOs towards women's rights seemed to be guided by their religious beliefs. They opined that Islam has already given equal rights to women and the current situation is because of a lack of religious education. The following comments are instructive:

> We believe that there is only one solution to such problems and that is education. If religious education which means the knowledge of Quran is properly given to people I believe such problems can be solved.
>
> The rights that Islam has given to women should be given to them.
>
> I only support those rights which are provided by the *Shariah*.
>
> I would prefer to invest in religious education so that we could make women aware of their religious rights. The talk about women's rights, which we have today in our society, is a western phenomenon. The West has made a woman a showpiece to exhibit. It does not give any protection to them. I think the kind of women's rights that have been given by Islam, if we propagate them properly the issue of women's rights can be easily solved.
>
> If you see history you will come to know that women were subjugated in the times of ignorance before Islam, and in principle Islam rejected such discrimination.
>
> In the Indian subcontinent, women have never been given equal rights. Those women who have education fight for their rights but they are very few in number. The situation of women in villages is really the worst. Men consider them slaves. It is because of this that they do violence to them, as they think that women are their property and they can do anything to them.

What follows from the above comments is that the principal conception of women's rights is based on religious orthodoxy. This is due to the prevalence of semi-feudal patriarchal social structures that give a distinct identity to women and their role within society. There are many elements in this identity construction but three stand out: the Islamic religion, patriarchal family traditions, and the gender relationships that are so often implicated in religious and family matters. Religion becomes important for men wishing to maintain their family traditions. In this context, the overlap of family traditions and religion is observable, where male-dominated family traditions are justified in the name of religion and the religious education of women becomes a priority.

Some CEOs, however, pointed out that no organization has ever approached them to ask for support in addressing such issues. Commenting on this, a CEO stated: 'We would most certainly want to support women's rights issues but there has to be someone to guide us. No such organization working on women's rights issues has ever approached us.' The comment indicates the need for civil society to engage the corporate sector in women's rights issues.

Human rights

Human rights violations in Pakistan are frequent. The Human Rights Commission of Pakistan (HRCP) is probably the only organization that prepares a comprehensive annual report on the state of human rights in Pakistan. According to the HRCP 2012 annual report, harassment of and violence against ethnic and religious minorities has continued. At least 583 people were killed and 853 injured in 213 incidents of sectarian-related terrorist attacks and clashes. Around 20 Ahmedis (a religious minority) were killed because of their religious identity. Six churches in Karachi were attacked. The land mafia in the city of Mardan in Khyber Pakhtunkhwa province demolished the 150-year old Baba Karam Singh temple (a Sikh temple). At least 14 journalists were killed in 2012 and Pakistan was considered the deadliest country for journalists, with a ranking of 151 out of 179 countries reported by the Press Freedom Index (HRCP 2012). As many as 913 girls and women were killed in the name of honour in 2012, of whom 99 were minors. In just the first six months of 2012 there were 1,573 recorded incidents of child sexual abuse (HRCP 2012).

It is not surprising therefore, that human rights was the second priority area for companies in Pakistan after the health sector. Around 29.8 per cent of companies support human rights issues, as shown in Table 7.11.

For support by industry, see Table 7.12.

It is important to note, however, that the United Nations Charter of Human Rights did not guide the view of human rights held by most of the companies. This was close to the concept of *Haqook-ul-Ibaad* (rights of fellow human beings) implicit in Islam. Overall, company CEOs and other senior officials were of the view that Islam defined human rights according to the principle of human goodwill, and the relationship of human beings according

Table 7.11 Support for human rights

Support	No.	Percentage
Yes	45	29.8
No	106	70.2
Total	151	100

Table 7.12 Support for human rights by industrial sector

Industry	Yes	No	Total
Leather	2	3	5
Food & Beverages	1	3	4
Trading	29	42	71
Auto Allied	2	8	10
Advertising/Print	0	3	3
Textiles	4	11	15
Sport	2	11	13
Services	1	11	12
Chemicals	0	5	5
Surgical	1	4	5
Electronics	1	1	2
Pharmaceutical	0	2	2
Construction	0	1	1
Other	2	1	3

to the principles of equality and justice. Human freedom and liberty is emphasized in the context of the status given by God to human beings, i.e. of *ashraful makhluqat* (greatest of all other creations including angels). This is because all other creations by God lack free will and knowledge of their existence. They lack the ability to take conscious, independent decisions. Their actions are either predetermined (as in the case of angels) or based on instinct (as is the case with animals). It is only human beings who can make choices and differentiate because God has given them mind and will power. They should not give this up to any tyrant.

Liberty and freedom, choice and differentiation are thus absent in all other creatures and it is these that distinguish human beings from the rest of creation. Freedom is the golden framework within which human beings rise to the noble height of their humanity and is the essence of the Islamic faith. Human liberty on the other hand implies the recognition of various rights and duties pertaining to belief, religion, thought, expression, work and behaviour. A CEO commented that Islam has given a number of rights to human beings, such as the individual's right to freedom, the right to justice, equality amongst human beings, the right to protest, freedom of expression, freedom of association, respect for other religions, the right to the basic necessities of life and equality before the law. The set of rights he identified does not clash with the

Universal Declaration of Human Rights, but was justified in the name of Islam.

Others professed that Islam offers an exceptionally well-developed social welfare system, which promotes an atmosphere of mutual concord among members of society. Islam accords dignity to human beings through the equitable distribution of wealth so that everyone in society can live a respectable life. A CEO commented: 'within the Islamic system, people receive equal opportunities and protection against unemployment, disease, infirmity and permanent widowhood'.

In most cases, the view of human rights upheld by CEOs and other senior officials was the outcome not of an in-depth study of Islam but of knowledge gained through experience and to an extent their exposure to contemporary information about human rights via (mainly) human rights NGOs and the media. While the officials of those companies that supported human rights projects strongly supported human rights issues in general, some were conservative when it came to the issue of women's rights. To paraphrase one CEO, Islam strongly preaches the protection of women's chastity and honour, and the Western notion of women's rights can lead to vulgarity and dishonour women.

Child labour/children's rights

There is an endemic problem of violence against children and child labour in Pakistan. According to the Human Rights Commission of Pakistan's 2012 annual report, around 1,573 incidents of child sexual abuse were recorded in the first six months of 2012. The provincial analysis showed that:

> Punjab continued to take the lead in the number of reported child abuse incidents recorded at 1,092, followed by 314 cases reported from Sindh, 62 from Khyber Pakhtunkhwa and 52 from the federal capital Islamabad, 33 from Balochistan, 16 cases were reported from Azad Jammu and Kashmir and 4 from Gilgit. In the preceding year, Sahil had reported a total of 2,942 child sexual abuse cases.
>
> (HRCP 2012)

Furthermore, there were around 7,000 reported cases of child kidnapping and 3,090 cases of child abduction in the city of Karachi alone (HRCP 2012). According to statistics provided by the Lahore police, a media report showed that 41 children were kidnapped between January 1 and November 5, 2012; 20 children up to the age of 14 were kidnapped for ransom, of which two were killed. Around 15 victims were recovered, two returned home on their own and one was yet to the retrieved (HRCP 2012).

Regarding child labour, there are no current statistics available in Pakistan. According to the latest Human Rights Report in Pakistan (HRCP 2012), an official survey of child labour was not carried out in 2012, despite commitments by the Pakistan Bureau of Statistics in 2011. Pakistan's last survey was

Table 7.13 Support for child labour prevention/children's rights by industrial sector

	Yes	No	Total
Industrial sectors			
Leather	1	4	5
Food & Beverages	2	2	4
Trading	4	67	71
Auto Allied	1	9	10
Advertising/Print	0	3	3
Textiles	0	15	15
Sport	2	11	13
Services	0	12	12
Chemicals	0	5	5
Surgical	1	4	5
Electronics	1	1	2
Pharmaceutical	0	2	2
Construction	0	1	1
Other	1	2	3
Total	13	138	151

conducted in 1996. According to the US Labour Department, Pakistan is one of the 27 countries out of 144 that have failed to remove the worst forms of child labour (HRCP 2012). According to unofficial estimates, almost 10 million children were involved in child labour in Pakistan. SPARC claimed that nearly 1.5 million children were engaged in child labour in Khyber Pakhtunkhwa alone (HRCP 2012).

Child labour and children's rights are therefore vital human rights issues that have yet to attract the attention of the corporate sector in Pakistan. Most companies did not recognize the importance of this area and only 8.6 per cent were found to be extending support to the cause of child labour prevention and children's rights in Pakistan. A breakdown of support for child labour prevention/children's rights by industry is given in Table 7.13.

Environmental protection

Water contamination, the depletion of forests for commercial use, air pollution, the widespread illegal hunting of endangered migratory birds such as bustards and Siberian cranes, inefficient waste management and climate change are some of the vitally important environmental issues confronting the people of Pakistan. Although government officials pay lip service to environmental protection and sustainable development, no significant measures to curb hazardous development are evident. Most development planning is lopsided, with grave environmental consequences. The corporate sector also seems to be neglecting this issue and the percentage of companies that supported environmental issues was no more than 3.3 per cent of the total sample. A breakdown of support for environmental matters by industry is given in Table 7.14:

Table 7.14 Support for environmental protection projects by industrial sector

Industry	Awareness regarding environment pollution control	Clean environment	Total
Trading	0	1	1
Sports	1	0	1
Chemicals	0	1	1
Other	0	2	2
Total	1	4	5

Water supply and sanitation

Water supply and sanitation face several challenges in Pakistan. Though 92 per cent of people have access to drinking water, this water is not safe to drink. Around 88 per cent of water supply schemes in Pakistan provide water that contains microbiological contamination (*The Tribune*, May 15, 2012). According to a Government of Pakistan official document, contamination from arsenic, nitrate and fluoride was detected in drinking water in various localities in Pakistan (GoP 2004). Moreover, water pressure is generally low in the water supply systems. Combined with leaky pipes, this leads to the infiltration of contaminated water.

The sanitation system also faces several difficulties. The quality of service is poor because of limited wastewater treatment. Poor drinking water quality and sanitation cause waterborne diseases (Bridges 2007). Millions of people become infected with waterborne diseases (Weekly Independent 2005).

Inadequate sanitation services have an economic impact that the World Bank estimated cost US$5.7 billion (almost 4 per cent of GDP) in 2006 (World Bank 2011b). Around 87 per cent of the impact is on health, while increased water supply costs represent 5 per cent; 8 per cent is on other areas. The health impacts lead to premature mortality and productivity losses, followed by treatment costs. The costs incurred regarding water supply are due to the high cost of supplying piped and bottled water and treating household water. Moreover, poor sanitation leads to poor environmental conditions that have significant economic costs (Nishat 2013).

Against the background of this situation regarding water supply and sanitation, 17.2 per cent of companies surveyed supported water supply and 13 per cent sanitation projects (see Table 7.15). Major outbreaks of waterborne diseases swept the cities of Faisalabad, Karachi, and Lahore in 2006 and most companies that supported water supply and sanitation projects were from these cities. The majority of companies, however, were from Karachi, where problems of water supply and sanitation are critical.

Though most companies were cognizant of the need for the provision of quality drinking water and better sanitation facilities – the absence of which

Table 7.15 Support for water supply and sanitation

Support	Water supply		Sanitation	
	No.	*Percentage*	*No.*	*Percentage*
Yes	26	17.2	13	8.6
No	125	82.8	138	91.4
Total	151	100	151	100

leads to endemic health problems and deteriorating environmental conditions – the CEOs and other senior officials were of the view that they did not have sufficient funds to adequately address these mega-issues. In their view, provision of such services is essentially the state's responsibility and there is a need to apply political pressure on the state to deliver in providing such essential amenities.

Income generation and microfinance

Around 58.7 million of the 180 million people in Pakistan are living below the poverty line (SDPI 2012). This means that every third Pakistani is living below the poverty line. Fifty-two per cent of people in Balochistan, 33 per cent in Sindh, 32 per cent in Khyber Pakhtunkhwa and 19 per cent in Punjab are extremely poor. Moreover, three million Pakistanis are unemployed (SDPI 2012). Poverty and unemployment were further increased significantly by three major natural disasters: the earthquake in 2005 and then floods in 2010 and 2011.

Overall, alleviating poverty through income generation is the biggest development challenge still to attract significant attention from the corporate sector in Pakistan. Only 8.6 percent and 2.6 percent of companies were found to be supporting income generation programs and microfinance projects, respectively. For a breakdown by industry, see Table 7.16.

Following the awarding of the 2006 Nobel Peace Prize to Muhammad Yunus, the founder of the Bangladeshi microcredit revolution, microcredit programmes have gained legitimacy in the international arena as a grassroots, bottom-up approach to development that can 'help the poor help themselves'. In Pakistan, too, the microfinance movement has gathered momentum and, according to recent data on microfinance in Pakistan, microfinance loans of US$508.2 million were dispersed to 2.9 million borrowers in 2012/13 (Palistan Market Profile 2014). International donors and civil society organizations have been particularly active in this area. CEOs and other senior officials of the companies contributing to microfinance projects were of the view that more awareness needs to be created within the corporate sector regarding the effectiveness of microfinance for poverty alleviation. Some opined that there is a need for organized joint ventures between the corporate sector, international donors, the government and civil society organizations to enhance the microfinance movement in Pakistan.

Table 7.16 Support for microcredit by industrial sector

Industry	Income generation			Microfinance		
	Yes	No	Total	Yes	No	Total
Leather	0	5	5	0	5	5
Food & Beverages	2	2	4	1	3	4
Trading	4	67	71	1	70	71
Auto Allied	0	10	10	1	9	10
Advertising/Print	0	3	3	0	3	3
Textiles	1	14	15	0	15	15
Sport	1	12	13	0	13	13
Services	0	12	12	0	12	12
Chemicals	1	4	5	0	5	5
Surgical	0	5	5	0	5	5
Electronics	1	1	2	1	1	2
Pharmaceutical	0	2	2	0	2	2
Construction	1	0	1	0	1	1
Other	2	1	3	0	3	3
Total	13	138	151	4	147	151

Table 7.17 Support for other projects by industrial sector

Industry	Financial aid for the needy	Monthly grocery/supplies	Workers' welfare	Clothing for the poor	Total
Leather	2	1	1	0	5
Food & Beverages	1	0	1	0	2
Trading	30	21	2	1	54
Auto Allied	6	3	0	0	9
Advertising/Print	2	1	0	0	3
Textiles	5	3	3	0	12
Sport	4	2	0	0	7
Services	7	4	0	0	11
Chemicals	2	2	0	0	4
Surgical	2	1	1	0	4
Electronics	1	0	0	0	1
Pharmaceutical	1	1	0	0	2
Construction	1	0	0	0	1
Other	0	0	1	0	1
Total	64	39	9	1	113

Support for other projects

A considerable number of companies, 113 (74.83 per cent), support other projects, such as financial aid for the needy, monthly grocery/supplies, workers' welfare, and clothing for the poor. The largest number (42 per cent) supported financial aid for the needy; this was followed by monthly grocery/supplies for the poor (25.8 per cent), workers' welfare (6 per cent) and clothing for the poor (0.7 per cent). Most giving in this category is one-off charity. Moreover, support in such areas is demand- and not supply-based – that is, it is not planned support. Support is usually offered on the recommendation of CEOs' relatives, company employees or individuals already known to the CEOs. The support is usually extended to people in the vicinity of company operations. See a breakdown by industry in Table 7.17).

Support for multiple areas in development/welfare

The survey reveals that, while a particular development issue might be prioritized by a company, most companies give their support to multiple development areas. Table 7.18 provides details of the support offered to multiple development projects by industrial sector.

According to the data, traders lead in extending support for social and developmental purposes. The largest share of corporate giving is by the trading community. It is difficult to understand the precise reasons for this; space does not permit the inclusion of comments by all the heads of trading companies. However, some of the comments permit it to be argued that manufacturing in Pakistan depends on traders for import and export; traders are linked to international markets, have more exposure to the world and are more aware of CSR.

Correlation between the areas of support and CSR policies of companies in Pakistan

As shown in Figure 7.1, of the 27.2 per cent of companies with a CSR policy, the highest percentage of companies that had CSR policy (22 per cent written and 35 per cent unwritten policies) supported health sector. Second to health, the greatest percentage of companies that had CSR policies was supporting the education sector (16 per cent written and 12 per cent unwritten policies). Next to education sector, the greatest percentage of companies having CSR policies were extending support in areas such as human rights, water supply and children rights. This shows that support in the above areas is more organized.

Target beneficiaries

The companies' definitions of CSR determined their target beneficiaries. As indicated in Figure 7.2, 30 per cent of companies considered their employees to be their target beneficiaries. These were the companies that defined CSR as 'employees' welfare'. Fifty-three per cent of companies identified their target beneficiaries as communities throughout the country and 17 per cent as communities in nearby areas. These were the companies that defined CSR as 'community welfare'. When asked which group of people they focus on as

Table 7.18 Support for multiple areas by industrial sector

Industry	Health	Education	Women welfare	Women's rights	Human rights	Child labour/ children's rights	Water supply	Sanitation	Income generation	Micro-finance	Environment	Other
Leather	2	0	0	0	2	1	1	1	0	0	0	5
Food & Beverages	2	3	1	0	1	2	3	3	2	1	0	2
Trading	13	10	4	3	29	4	10	5	4	1	1	54
Auto Allied	2	1	0	0	2	1	1	1	0	1	0	9
Advertising/Print	1	0	0	0	0	0	0	0	0	0	0	3
Textiles	8	4	0	0	4	0	2	1	1	0	0	12
Sport	8	6	0	0	2	2	2	0	1	0	1	7
Services	1	2	0	0	1	0	1	0	0	0	0	11
Chemicals	2	0	0	0	0	0	12	0	1	0	1	4
Surgical	2	0	0	0	1	1	2	0	0	0	0	4
Electronics	1	0	0	0	1	1	0	1	1	1	0	1
Pharmaceutical	0	0	0	0	0	0	0	0	0	0	0	2
Construction	0	0	0	0	0	0	1	0	0	0	0	1
Other	3	1	0	1	2	1	2	1	2	0	2	1
Total	45	28	5	4	44	13	26	13	13	4	5	116

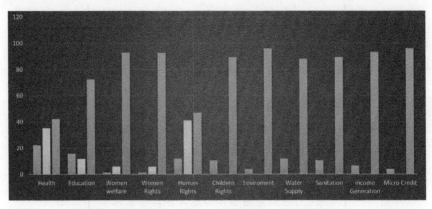

Figure 7.1 Sector wise information about companies CSR policy

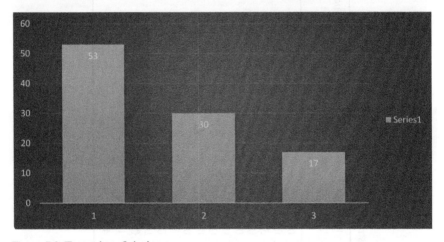

Figure 7.2 Target beneficiaries

target beneficiaries within communities, most of the companies said that they targetted the poorest of the poor.

What do CEOs say about their target beneficiaries?

For CSR we feel that the corporate sector should involve its business houses and actively participate in community building to specifically support the under-privileged segment of society and our company specifically supports youth in such communities as they are our future.

I have been trying to work for community development. It has been my top priority so that community building culture is developed.

Employees' welfare is important but the most important is community welfare. The corporate sector cannot develop unless society develops.

Therefore community development is an area within the vast ambit of CSR which is of supreme importance.

We spend 10 per cent of our earning on community development which we believe is linked with our own development as well.

Possible benefits to companies from their engagement with social welfare/development projects

Twenty-and-a-half per cent of companies got significant benefit from investing in development/welfare projects, 15.9 per cent benefited 'equally' (i.e. benefited across the board in terms of image-building, tax benefits, public goodwill and personal satisfaction), 12.6 benefited insignificantly, 15.9 per cent did not benefit at all, for 32.5 per cent it did not matter and 2.6 per cent of companies did not know whether they got any benefit in terms of image-building (for other areas, see Table 7.19) This data indicates what CEOs and other senior officials thought about the benefits they got in terms of, for example, image-building because of their contribution to development/welfare causes. It does not tell us anything about their planned investments for image-building.

Conclusions

The issue of having a corporate social policy is crucial and a higher percentage of companies with formal CSR policies, especially written policies, is a good indicator of the extent to which the corporate sector is investing for development in an organized manner. However, in a developing country such as Pakistan, where CSR initiatives are at an embryonic stage, it is difficult to expect that a great number of companies would practice CSR in an organized manner. It is not surprising, therefore, that in Pakistan overall only 27.2 per cent of companies had a CSR policy, of which 63.4 per cent were written and 36.6 per cent were unwritten but formal. In the main it was large national companies that had written policies. The main reasons identified for not

Table 7.19 Possible benefits to companies

	Image building		Tax benefits		Public goodwill	
	No.	*%*	*No.*	*%*	*No.*	*%*
Benefited significantly	31	20.5	12	8	22	14.6
Benefited equally	24	15.9	32	21	42	27.8
Benefited insignificantly	19	12.6	22	15	18	11.9
No benefit	24	15.9	23	15	21	13.9
Does not matter	49	32.5	56	37	45	29.8
Do not know	4	2.6	6	4	3	2
Total	151	100	151	100	151	100

having a written CSR policy that could lead to more organized CSR activity were lack of resources, motivation and interest. Though the percentage of companies with a CSR policy (especially written policy) is not significant, it could be argued that in a society where the economy is largely unregulated even this percentage is a welcome sign.

Whether companies opt for written CSR policies in the long run will depend on awareness raising and more involvement by civil society organizations and the role of the state in regulating the economy and providing companies with an enabling environment through various public sector instruments. Proper accounting and auditing, for example, might encourage companies to report their contribution to a social cause and thus prefer written CSR policies.

The research also shows that in most cases the decision-making regarding CSR is centralized and it is CEOs who take decisions. This trend is more pronounced in companies that do not have a written CSR policy. In the companies with written policies, in which corporate giving is institutionalized to some extent, the situation is a little different. In such companies, the decision-making is to some extent decentralized.

The tendency for CEOs to take the decisions about CSR was found to extend to implementation as well. In a majority of companies the CEO not only makes the decisions about social investment but implements them as well. Of the companies in which CEOs make the decisions, only a few (8 per cent) had a written policy; a majority (63 per cent) were found to be having an informal/unwritten CSR policy. This seems to be another indicator that modern forms of CSR have yet to be embedded in Pakistan.

Regarding priority areas for development, health and education were considered more important than areas such as the environment, women's rights, children's rights, water supply, sanitation, income generation and microcredit. However, it is interesting to note that the corporate sector in Pakistan is not unaware of its responsibilities regarding 'rights-orientated advocacy work' to do with basic human rights. After the health sector, human rights were the next priority area of support. Nevertheless, in most cases it was religious notions of rights that informed CEOs' views and as a result some CEOs seemed conservative in relation to women's rights and followed their own interpretation of such rights in Islam. It is therefore difficult to categorize their attitude towards corporate giving as based on modern principles of development that takes into account the environment and the modern interpretation of human rights to deal with the consequences of inequality and injustice with humans and nature. It was rather that of welfare.

It was important to note that most companies (73.3 per cent) were of the view that the major benefit they got out of their social investment was spiritual in nature, guided by the Islamic religion. The basic motivation was, therefore, to satisfy the obligatory Islamic requirement to make charitable donations. There were others who identified public goodwill and company image-building as significant benefits to be had from their involvement in social projects. On the whole, corporate philanthropy remains a dominant aspect of corporate social responsibility in Pakistan.

Note

1 It is important to mention here that the question regarding areas of support was multiple-choice, allowing respondents to select more than one option if they preferred.

8   Channels and forms of support

Channels of support are an important variable that governs the extent to which companies employ their resources in an organized manner. For example, companies that prefer using intermediate professional bodies, such as NGOs or foundations/trusts, provide their support in a much more organized manner than when they themselves approach the end beneficiaries.

Information about forms of support gives insight into company preferences and reasons behind choices between various forms of monetary and non-monetary support. This chapter analyzes indigenous companies' preferences in this area of channels and forms of support. An analysis of the correlation between channels of support and companies' CSR policies is also presented. For this purpose, corporate organizations were asked a multiple-choice question which allowed respondents more than one option regarding preferred channels and forms of support.

Channels of support

As shown in Figure 8.1, 95.4 per cent of companies preferred supporting end beneficiaries directly, 16.6 per cent provided support through their own welfare organizations/trusts or other trusts or foundations, and 16.6 per cent of companies worked in partnership with NGOs. About 27.6 per cent of companies provided support through all these channels.

Support for end beneficiaries

As shown above, the majority of companies prefer to directly support end beneficiaries; such support is not very organized – in most cases it is demand-based and one-off. Support through companies' own welfare organization/ trusts or other trusts supported by companies or NGOs is much more organized and likely to be carried out on a long-term basis. It was found that in most cases companies lacked trust in intermediary professional NGOs dependent on foreign funding. To paraphrase a comment by a CEO of a large national company: 'We prefer to support directly to end beneficiaries because we are sure that the funds will reached to the right people.' Another comment by a

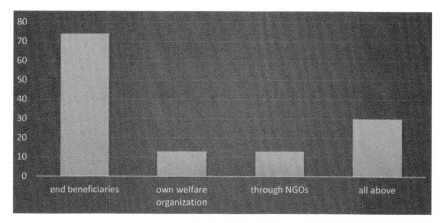

Figure 8.1 Channel of support

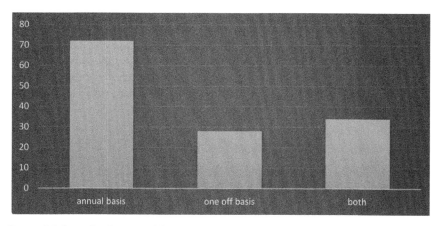

Figure 8.2 Length of partnership

CEO is instructive: 'In my opinion it is important to give charity to the end beneficiaries, as nowadays there are many professionals/professional organizations that collect charity in the name of social welfare but most of it does not reach the poor.'

A few companies revealed their view that if they worked through an NGO, half the amount they wished to invest in some social cause would be consumed by the NGO to maintain its structure. Commenting on this, one CEO remarked:

> There are so many problems people are facing that it will be enough contribution to solve a few of them instead of investing on NGOs structures, salaries of their staff, office rents and other administrative costs.

Some other reasons revealed by companies are:

We want to meet and see the person getting our support.

In such cases the CEO himself, his family or another senior official extend support to those who are personally known to them. The reason again is that this way, the funds donated would reach the right people:

We get satisfaction in working directly with end beneficiaries.

Some companies' CEOs felt that on an individual as well as on a family level, they get spiritual satisfaction when donating directly to end beneficiaries, especially when they see that such beneficiaries have to some extent resolved problems as a result of this support:

NGOs have never approached us.

Some companies did not restrict themselves to work only for end beneficiaries. However, they said that no intermediary organizations/NGOs had ever approached them to inform them about their development projects/programmes. These companies opined that they didn't have enough information about NGOs' work in Pakistan. If NGOs ever approached them they would like to work through them, assuming the NGOs had credibility.

Working through own welfare organizations/ trusts

Several companies that are doing charitable/philanthropic work in an organized manner have established their own welfare organizations or trusts. Companies revealed that they had established such setups to be able to work on a large scale and also work directly with end beneficiaries. It also assured them that their funds were utilized properly and reaching the right people/communities.

Some companies also run their own foundations or support trusts/foundations run by the non-profit sector. Two prominent examples are the Hashoo Foundation and the Citizens Foundation (TCF) in Pakistan. To understand their work a short description of their programmes is in order.[1]

The Hashoo Foundation

The Hashoo Group, established in 1960 by Saddaruddin Hashwani, founded the Hashoo Foundation in 1988. The Hashoo Group is one of the larger conglomerates in Pakistan. It does business in cotton trading, hospitality, oil and gas exploration and production, information technology, investments, minerals, ceramics, pharmaceuticals, travel and tourism, real estate and commodity trading. The Hashoo Group includes Pearl Continental Hotels, Marriott Hotels and Orient Petroleum International.

The Hashoo Foundation contributes to human development and poverty alleviation in Pakistan through its programme in the areas of economic development, education, skills development and humanitarian assistance. It also runs a skills training project for urban Afghan refugees.

ECONOMIC DEVELOPMENT

The Hashoo Foundation's economic development programme has three components: 1) the Women's Empowerment through Honey Bee Farming Project, 2) the Expanded Dairy Development Project and 3) the Marble Shine Association. With the purpose of empowering women in the northern areas of Pakistan through honey bee farming, the first project was initiated in 2007. The aim was to expand home-based women's entrepreneurship.

The project links women to the value chain of the honey market within Pakistan by buying their produce on condition that the women send their children to quality schools, take care of their health, have regular health check-ups and improve nutrition at home. This results in an overall improved quality of life for women, children and their families. The women who have been involved in the project feel empowered by their integration into an enterprise that was mainly male-dominated. This project is, therefore, successfully addressing the gender gap in terms of income generation opportunities for women in Pakistan. Other outcomes of the project are also exemplary:

- Eighty per cent of the honey producers are associated with the Northern Areas Honey Bee Keepers Welfare Association and the president of the association is a woman.
- Thirty per cent of the women have expanded their honey bee farming business.
- More than 1,000 children are attending school because of this project.
- Beekeepers are spending 69 per cent of their income from honey bee farming on the education of their children, 10 per cent on better nutrition for their families and 30 per cent on healthcare expenses.
- The project has helped women by selling 31,000 kilograms of their honey between 2007 and 2011.
- There has been a 32 per cent increase in average household income.
- The production of honey has increased from 16 to 18 kilograms per hive.
- Some 642 beekeepers have received training in beekeeping in Gilgit-Baltistan and Khyber Pakhtunkhwa (KPK).
- While there are 642 direct beneficiaries, more than 5,000 dependents are benefiting from honey projects.

The Expanded Dairy Development Project (EDDP) is designed to educate the local community in how to improve the breed of local cattle, increase the production of milk through better fodder and livestock management, improve care and treatment of livestock by training veterinary extension workers, set up a chilling unit for collection of milk from farmers, produce quality products like cheese, butter and yogurt for income generation and install and use bio-gas for heating and cooking. The project is expanded by funding provided by the Church World Services and EED.

This project builds on the success of the Sustainable Livelihood for Women-Headed Households project. The lessons learnt and connections made with the livestock department through this project have proved to be key to the success of the EDDP.

The third phase of the project will involve extending EDDP by setting up a marketing mechanism for the EDDP's dairy projects, and branding and franchising the dairy products for sale and distribution, targeting a mass market.

Finally, the Marble Shine Association (MSA) offers high-quality floor polishing services to commercial, government and private clients and is a revenue-generating arm of the Hashoo Foundation. The services provided by MSA contribute to the operating costs of the Hashoo Foundation.

The Association employs and trains more than 70 staff. More than 1,000 workers trained by MSA are earning their livelihood through employment or running their own enterprises. MSA works with five-star hotel chains, private hospitals and governmental facilities, as well as commercial buildings.

EDUCATION PROGRAMME

The Hashoo Foundation's education programme comprises four sub-programmes: 1) the Child Education Support Programme (CESP), 2) Hashoo Foundation Schools (HFS), 3) Early Childhood Development Training and 4) the Scholarship Programme.

The Child Education Support Programme (CESP) was started in 2004. The programme has contributed significantly to the high-quality education of children who would otherwise lack access to such facilities in remote areas of northern Pakistan and in the city of Rawalpindi. Community leaders' support is obtained for the identification of deserving children, who are then enrolled in 120 schools established by the Agha Khan Education Service Pakistan (AKESP). The Hashoo Foundation covers the cost of tuition fees, books, shoes, stationery and uniforms.

Access to quality education is a priority for the Hashoo Foundation. Since 2004, their Child Education Support Programme (CESP) has helped improve access to quality education for children in some of the most isolated parts of Pakistan. Operating initially in the Northern Areas, CESP provides financial support to out-of-school children. These children are identified with the help of community leaders. They are then enrolled into one of the 120 schools established by AKESP. Hashoo Foundation pays for their tuition fees and provides them with books, shoes, stationery and a uniform. The same model is now followed in the region of Rawalpindi.

The Foundation has also established its own schools and manages a network of ten primary schools in extremely poor, remote areas where access to even primary-level education is problemmatical. British Petroleum supports four of these schools, under their Corporate Social Responsibility programme.

The Hashoo Foundation's Early Childhood Development (ECD) programme builds the capacity of teachers to be able to provide high-quality student-centered education involving interactive teaching methodologies in a society where a student-centered mode of teaching is still not prevalent and where corporal punishment is the norm. The teacher training adopted by ECD, employing interactive and humane approaches to teaching, involves: 1) sessions based on practical activities as well as theory, 2) hands-on training in a classroom environment, and 3) summer camps involving parents and children.

In addition to the above, the Hashoo Foundation runs a scholarship programme. Talented students unable to afford higher education are supported throughout their studies at university. This helps deserving students get out of the poverty trap and gain better employment opportunities. A new policy being introduced by the Foundation encourages scholars funded by them to contribute to the programme once they enter worthwhile employment after their studies.

SKILLS DEVELOPMENT PROGRAMME

The Hashoo Foundation's skills development programme is divided into three components: 1) a vocational training programme, 2) life skills training and 3) career mentor training. The vocational training programme conducts regular market research identifying vocational training needs and organizes and conducts structured vocational training creating linkages between young job seekers and job markets, nationally and internationally. The life skills training programme enables young men and women to increase their professional competence. Life skills involve interpersonal and psychosocial skills for informed decision-making, effective communication and self-management skills for leading a productive life. This training is offered by the Foundation through its Human Development Resource Centres located in Rawalpindi, Chitral and Gilgit.

Similarly, the Career Mentoring Programme is a work-based mentoring and learning initiative. It provides opportunities to graduates to assist in their development and the management of their careers. A mentor is appointed for each student for two months for an internship and a month for voluntary work. Hashoo Foundation initiated the Life Skills training program in 2006 to enable young Pakistani men and women to make the most of their professional competence. Life skills refer to a large group of psycho-social and interpersonal skills which can help people make informed decisions, communicate effectively, and develop self-management skills that may help them lead a healthy and productive life. These trainings are offered by the Foundation through its Human Development Resource Centers located in Rawalpindi, Chitral and Gilgit.

The mentors' qualifications and experiences are matched with students' aspirations. Training offered under this programme covers: job-hunting skills, resumé-writing skills, hotel management and tourism, English language, information and communication technology, office management and secretarial training, communication skills, leadership skills, decision-making skills, conflict resolution skills, pedagogical training, school management and leadership. The programme also provides a diploma in Montessori teaching and certification and short courses in early childhood development and education (ECD&E).

HUMANITARIAN ASSISTANCE PROGRAMME

The Humanitarian Assistance Programme is an important innovation given the absence of state-sponsored social safety nets. It helps vulnerable families and individuals facing temporary hardship or unforeseen expenditures that can throw them into a long-term cycle of poverty. The programme supports vulnerable families and individuals through medical, financial and educational assistance. It helps the extremely poor to overcome critical situations before they are further exacerbated.

The Hashoo Foundation also provides emergency relief to the victims of natural and human disasters. It significantly helped the victims of the earthquake of 2005, the internally displaced persons (IDPs) crisis in 2009, and the floods of 2010.

As part of its Humanitarian Assistance Programme, the Hashoo Foundation initiated another project called the 'Sahara Fund'. In Pakistan, companies such as news organizations, hotels, private security firms and even fast food outlets face terrorist threats on a daily basis (Syed 2010). On September 20, 2008, a suicide bomb blast hit the Islamabad Marriott Hotel, killing 56 people and injuring more than 260. Some of those injured were left disabled. Sarah Hashwani, chairperson of the Hashoo Foundation, was moved by the critical situation of the 600 or so immediate family members of victims and launched the Sahara Fund. Since then the Fund has provided medical care for the injured and helped the families of the victims through support for their children's education, medical needs, skills training, and employment to make them self-sufficient. Each family's situation was individually assessed so they could be helped to achieve the same income level that they had prior to the explosion.

The Foundation also established a basic health unit in Talhatta, Balakot. Its purpose was to help vulnerable communities affected by natural as well as man-made disasters by providing emergency health relief services. These services were first offered during the catastrophic earthquake of 2005, providing relief to the earthquake-affected victims of Talhatta. Following the remarkable success of this unit, the model was replicated by establishing the Hashoo Medical Centre in Gwadar, Balochistan in 2007, the Hassan Ali Hashwani Dispensary in Karachi in 2008, and a basic health unit for Afghan refugees in

Islamabad in 2010. The Foundation also provided much-needed relief to internationally displaced people in Swat (in Khyber Pakhtunkhwa province) through an emergency health unit (June 2009 – February 2010) in Charsadda, Khyber Pakhtunkhwa.

Another project initiated by the Humanitarian Assistance Programme was the Hashoo Foundation's Spinal Cord Injury Project for the rehabilitation of Pakistani earthquake victims. The project provides services to patients with spinal injuries: educational and vocational training, peer counselling, caregiver services, mobility equipment (wheelchairs, canes) and bladder care supplies. The training gives patients the opportunity to learn to live independently. Finally, the Hashoo Foundation runs a skills training project for urban Afghan refugees. This was started in 1999 and has provided training to hundreds of men and women to enable them to increase their income by taking advantage of both labour-market and self-employment opportunities.

The Citizens Foundation

A group of concerned citizens in Karachi, mainly businessmen, founded the Citizens Foundation in 1995. It was registered as a company limited by guarantee under Section 42 of the Companies Ordinance, 1984.

The Citizens Foundation (TCF) works in formal-sector education for unprivileged children, targetting the most deprived urban and rural communities. With so many localities crying out for help, TCF decided to build schools in areas ignored by both the government and the private sector. While all TCF schools maintain certain academic standards, equal attention is given to extra-curricular activities. Student trips to parks and other venues outside school are frequently organized. Moreover, special care is paid to children's health: the playgrounds are dedicated to sports activities and schools provide children with free snacks.

As of 2013, TCF has established 910 purpose-built schools nationwide. The enrolment total is 126,000. TCF endeavours to maintain gender equality by encouraging female enrolment and maintains a 50 per cent female student population on most of its campuses. The number of female faculty members in TCF schools is 6,300. TCF has also established two teacher training centres, in Karachi and Mansehra, dedicated to the ongoing development of their teaching faculty. About 9,500 jobs have been created in the communities in which TCF operates. It has become one of the leading organizations in the field of formal education in Pakistan providing education to the underprivileged. One of the major sources of TCF funding is the Pakistani corporate sector. For example, one of its major educational projects is the Aagahi Adult Literacy Programme, which provides education to women from rural areas and urban slums. National Foods, the Shield corporation and International Textile support the programme.

Corporate – NGOs partnership

Partnerships are emerging between NGOs and the corporate sector (as distinct from the private sector, which includes small and micro-enterprises) as large companies – and particularly multinational corporations (MNCs) – become increasingly concerned about the impact of their activities in less developed countries. Most companies now have voluntary codes of conduct on social and environmental issues, which they wish to see enacted in order to protect the values associated with their products from allegations that they are produced using exploitative or hazardous working practices. NGOs in turn recognize the increasing importance of companies in development, both locally and internationally, as private flows of direct foreign investment to developing countries increase, flows of official aid diminish and governments are less able to provide adequate services. Both businesses and NGOs see the need to move from a confrontational approach to one of collaboration – though without losing the freedom to be confrontational when necessary. The following account presents a picture of the indigenous corporate sector's collaboration with NGOs in Pakistan. The evolution of the industrial sector has been outlined in Chapter 4. Before providing an analysis of NGO collaboration with the indigenous corporate sector, it will be useful to have an overview of the NGO sector in Pakistan as well.

The state of NGOs in Pakistan: an overview

A few welfare NGOs have existed in Pakistan since independence and a few (such as Anjuman Hamayat-e-Islam) even existed before the partition of the Indian subcontinent. These were mostly 'non-political, private and voluntary organizations that worked either under the patronage or in close association with the government' (Jilani 1998: 100). Being mostly charitable and welfare organizations, they worked either for the general benefit of people or were related to particular ethnic or religious groups and worked to fulfill the welfare aims of such organizations (Jilani 1998: 100).

The terms 'civil society' and 'NGO' came into fashion when foreign-funded development NGOs emerged in the late 1980s. This move gave birth to NGOs that adopted rights-based approaches in their work. Even those foreign-funded NGOs that initiated service-oriented development and welfare work included rights-based approaches to their work as cross-cutting themes.

There is not much written on the history of these NGOs. Only a few studies exist: for example, one conducted by CIVICUS (World Alliance for Citizen's Participation) in collaboration with the Agha Khan Foundation and another by the Social Policy and Development Centre (SPDC) in collaboration with the Johns Hopkins University, USA, do provide a profile of these NGOs. The CIVICUS study also provides an overview of NGOs' political significance and contribution. The study that most explicitly (albeit briefly) addresses the history of development and human rights NGOs and their political significance in Pakistan was conducted by Jilani (1998). According to Jilani there are two types of development NGOs in Pakistan. The first type concentrates on service-orientated work such as microfinance and infrastructural development (mostly in the health and education sectors), while the second type adopt rights-based approaches in their work (Jilani 1998). I would add that many of the NGOs that provide services include rights-based approaches in their work. For example, for a considerable time such NGOs have been including gender equality as a cross-cutting theme in their service-orientated projects. Other NGOs purely do advocacy work on, for example, human rights, women's rights and children's rights issues. It is these NGOs (development and advocacy- or rights-based) that are now termed 'civil society' in Pakistan. They work in collaboration with transnational actors such as the United Nations and its associated agencies, the international financial institutions and international donor countries.

Which organizations in Pakistan can be defined as NGOs is contested. There are differences of opinion as to the nature of NGOs. For example, Zaidi (1999: 221) defines NGOs as those 'national, private, non-profit organizations that are involved in developmental work in underdeveloped countries and are not membership organizations; this term excludes northern NGOs'; whereas CIVICUS and SDPC's studies include all non-profit organizations that are registered with the government of Pakistan as NGOs. These studies do not make the distinctions of the above writers.

There is no reliable information available on the number of NGOs in Pakistan. SDPC's study has identified 45,000 and CIVICUS around 60,000 NGOs in Pakistan. These figures include all kinds of NGOs. As for the number of foreign-funded NGOs in the country, no reliable figure is available. According to CIVICUS, the impression that NGOs in Pakistan are 'heavily dependent on foreign funds may hold true for large development-oriented advocacy organizations' (Baig & Rabia 2001: 8). It is similarly difficult to estimate the total of NGO funding.

The significance of foreign funding has important implications for the sustainability of NGO projects, their accountability and their legitimacy. Since these NGOs and their projects are so largely dependent on the continuous flow of funds from foreign donors, it becomes difficult to sustain projects: sometimes, the organizations themselves or their partner community-based organizations (CBOs) are disbanded once the flow of funds ceases. One good example of this is the capacity-building projects in Pakistan. During the 1990s, most of the national-level big NGOs introduced capacity-building projects and created hundreds of community-based organizations (CBOs), especially in the rural and semi-urban areas. However, once the funding for capacity-building projects decreased, the NGOs that were sponsoring the local CBOs discontinued their capacity-building projects. Consequently, a number of CBOs had to end their work. Currently the flow of foreign funding is towards the issue of governance and all major NGOs in one way or another are involved in such projects.

The other implication is for the organizational environment and the nature of NGO accountability. Mercer points out that the 1990s was a decade in which a host of studies on NGOs praised their efforts in strengthening democracy, however a number of studies also accused civil society organizations of being 'often fragmented, unorganized, uncooperative and weak' (Mercer 2002: 13). He further elaborated that NGOs are often 'internally undemocratic; characterized by authoritarian or charismatic personalized leaderships; competitive; riven along class, gender, religious, regional, spatial and ethnic fault-lines; and steered by either the state or donors, or both' (Mercer 2002:13). This is true in the case of Pakistan as well. For example, many community members and NGO workers informed me in their interviews that the decision making in NGOs is usually a centralized affair in the hands of the chief executive officers, who are usually responsible for planning and implementation of plans for soliciting foreign funding. It is such executives and their assistants who typically do the major public relations work with international officials and foreign donors to get funds.

Mercer argues that most NGOs are primarily accountable to their funding sources and not to the local communities they work for. During my field research, most CBOs complained that the national level NGOs solicit resources from foreign donors on their behalf, and when the funding is not available they discontinue their projects. There is no mechanism through which local communities can make them accountable when a certain project is discontinued. Since the national-level NGOs are managing development projects through local CBOs, the ultimate pressure is placed on the latter, as they are in contact with the local communities and are held responsible for the discontinuation of the project.

The national-level NGOs, instead of experiencing this pressure, start making plans to solicit funds for new projects. Ali (2003: 51), with regard to NGOs, states that 'these NGOs generally have no constitution and no system of election, therefore also no accountability'. Since most foreign-funded NGOs are not membership-based organizations, the need to elect executives does not arise. This is mainly due to a lack of attention to local resource mobilization, which can only be successful through a large network of members with different sectors of society including the corporate sector.

In short, NGOs have not been very successful in creating an effective local base of supporters who will provide them with resources and real political support in their fight against underdevelopment and injustice in society. There is not the trust that they would continue their interest in issues due to the changing agendas and priorities of their donors or be ready to take on board input from below. It is commonly observed that only a small number of predictable supporters (mainly NGO workers and some of their already converted sympathizers) participate in NGO processions. Awareness of the precariousness of such a situation is gradually becoming evident within foreign-funded NGOs, but not many of them have decided to find alternative, local, sources of funding in order to create the network of friends/supporters necessary to acquire political legitimacy within the country. The reason is that NGOs are conditioned by the availability of funds from foreign donors. With the change in donor priorities, their projects are discontinued, which further harms the credibility of their work. Mobilizing local resources, especially from the corporate sector, will surely help NGOs gain credibility.

Working through NGOs

Most companies initiate development projects themselves or through cooperating with NGOs. NGOs are legal organizations that aim to be opinion leaders and pressure groups and initiate strategic changes by creating public awareness and response via advocacy campaigns. They are also significantly involved in service delivery in areas and sectors where the state has failed to deliver. On the other hand, private sector companies allocate resources for various social causes as well as for public relations activities. NGO and private sector cooperation in the implementation of CSR projects is important.

Internationally, various examples of NGO and business enterprises can be cited. For example, the Body Shop has been conducting a corporate social responsibility project with the collaboration of Amnesty International. The Body Shop and Amnesty International organized a 'Make your Mark' campaign to mark the 50th anniversary of the Universal Declaration of Human Rights. They 'collected more than three million thumbprints in 34 countries in support of 12 human rights campaigners who defend human rights in threatening conditions' (Manokha, 2004: 58, as cited in Karabulut and Demir 2006: 6). Similarly, Starbucks has worked with NGOs since 1996. Starbucks made an agreement to collaborate with the Ford Foundation and Oxfam America. Oxfam America is an NGO, part of Oxfam International. It focuses on projects related to poverty, hunger and social injustice around the world (Karabulut 2006: 7). Oxfam 'also shares its broader view of human rights with Starbucks' (Karabulut 2006: 7). Oxfam and Starbucks have developed greater mutual respect (Argenti 2004: 91, as cited in Karbulut 2006: 7). Similarly, in collaboration with the World Wide Fund for Nature in China, BP has supported environmental education in schools in China, with a multi-disciplinary approach. A formal agreement was signed between BP and the World Wide Fund for Nature in China to test environmental education materials and methodologies to bring about improvements in the primary and secondary school curriculum. The collaboration helped China 'integrate environmental education into national teacher-training programs in all subject areas. Students are encouraged to understand environmental issues and take action themselves' (Young 2002: 36, as cited in Karbulut 2006: 7).

Although there are not many, examples can also be found of NGO and corporate partnerships in Pakistan, the most prominent being between the Save the Children Fund and the sporting goods manufacturers represented by the Sialkot Chamber of Commerce and Industry (SCCI) in the city of Sialkot and their international partner brands – represented by the World Federation of Sporting Goods Industry – to eliminate child labour in the Sialkot sports industry.

However, as mentioned earlier, in most cases, indigenous corporate organizations seem to have a lack of confidence in NGOs, especially those that largely depend on funding from foreign sources. This is because of the perceptions that CEOs and other senior officials have of NGOs' credibility. The companies opined that most NGOs are not credible and the way they work is not transparent. As a result, they believed that the NGOs benefit more than the end beneficiaries. A variety of comments can be quoted:

> There is only little work done by NGOs. Our own members within the market and our families are doing more social work than NGOs. However, we do not publicize our contribution, as we believe in the saying that if you donate from one hand the other hand should not know about it. We donate in millions but we never tell about it to anyone.
>
> The entire society has become corrupted and NGOs are also part of it.
>
> I don't have a good impression of NGOs. One reason is that their transparency is always questionable and secondly it is not clear whether the funds they get are spent on the right cause. Apparently it seems that due to their own luxurious setups more funds are spent on their own selves than those in whose name they collect funds. It looks like a fashion and a means to collect funds, as no signs of their presence in this society in the form of development are visible. If NGOs had really worked then it should have been visible.

Through in-depth interviews of the CEOs of different companies it was learnt that the views of a majority of them were based on information they get from the media and through word of mouth and not any direct experience of working with NGOs. The following comments are important:

> Personally I do not have any experience of working with NGOs but often it is in newspapers that NGOs are working on a foreign agenda.
>
> More than 50 per cent of NGOs in Pakistan are such that work for the objectives of those who give them funds. Certain objectives are in front of us but certain are hidden. We never come to know about their real objectives.
>
> I never had any interaction with NGOs in the past. However based on news in different newspapers and other sources of information, it can be said that some organizations are doing good work but most of them are misusing funds.
>
> *Edhi* Foundation and *Al-Khidmat* is doing good work. As for foreign-funded NGOs we do not have much information about them. However, their impression is generally not good.

Some CEOs thought that NGOs' administrative expenses are too great and that therefore the real benefit does not go to the end beneficiaries. Some comments by CEOs and other senior officials are instructive:

> My opinion about NGOs is not good. There are only a few NGOs working with dedication. Around 90 per cent of NGOs are not utilizing funds properly. Their administrative costs are so high that they are doing welfare work only in name. If you visit their offices, you will see a huge number of staff with a number of vehicles they own and their rooms are fully air-conditioned. What all this reflects is that most funds are spent on them instead of development projects.
> Personally, I do not know much about NGOs. My perception however is that they spend a lot of money on the running of organization and administration and less on meeting their targets.
> NGOs' work comes in the sphere of social welfare. Those who are running NGOs therefore should earn their living from some other sources and not from the funds that they have. They are running NGOs like corporate bodies, which is not appropriate.

The issue of foreign funding solicited by NGOs has important repercussions. The most important is the potential it gives for detracters within the state and society (such as religious groups) to discredit NGOs as foreign agents propagating Western agendas. This significantly harms their credibility. In this context, Holloway (2001: 8) has argued that:

> Foreign funding makes you politically vulnerable to accusations that you are only doing the work because you are paid to do so, or because you are obeying the instructions of some foreign power that may have some concealed motives to the detriment of your country. Development is a political process and foreign funding provides ammunition to detractors – especially those in government – that you are being used politically by foreigners.

The validity of Holloway's argument in the case of Pakistan can be illustrated through the example of a series of attempts by the government, politically motivated religious groups and the government-manipulated media to discredit NGOs as foreign agents. For example, in 1996 the government put the Social Welfare Agencies (Registration & Regulation) bill before the Senate. This bill would 'eliminate civic education as a permissible CSO activity, thus precluding the advocacy role of CSOs. Although the bill was never made law, it did engender a strong sense of vulnerability among CSOs' (Baig & Rabia 2001: 13). The bill aimed to restrict NGOs' activities, especially those pertaining to advocacy and social and political education. Again, in 1998/9, there was an intense media campaign against NGOs and a subsequent de-registration of a significant number of NGOs by the government (around 2,500 in the Punjab alone). The accusation made by the government, the state media, a dominant part of the print media and extremist elements in society was that NGOs (especially women's and human rights organizations) in Pakistan were promoting Western values and pursuing a foreign agenda detrimental to the cultural fabric of Pakistani society. Recently (in December 2012), on a private channel, a prominent political leader accused NGOs giving polio vaccinations to poor children of acting as intelligence agencies for foreign donors (ARY News 2012). Such campaigns and propaganda further erode people's confidence in development and rights-based NGOs and harm their credibility. It becomes imperative therefore that NGOs, especially development and rights-based NGOs, start to build local networks of funding through a sustained effort to tap local resources. Local corporate resources are one possible option. Such endeavours have the potential to create awareness of the modern concept of CSR and build effective NGO-corporate sector partnerships.

Some companies, however, had positive views of NGOs. In their opinion, NGOs were contributing a lot and creating considerable awareness of people's problems in Pakistan. They believed that such work should be encouraged and extended further. A few comments by CEOs are instructive here:

> I think the work NGOs are doing is well-intentioned. They bring funds from other countries and spend on good projects here. Such work is done in almost all poor countries and we must not distrust foreign-funded NGOs.
>
> NGOs are significantly contributing towards society. Name any field, for example women's rights or any other, they are doing good work. Such work should be extended.
>
> NGOs are doing very good work but the issue is that the problems are numerous whereas resources available are limited. That's the reason that the impact of their work is not visible. NGOs are working on environmental issues, education, and sanitation and so on but due to the lack of resources their work is so segmented that it is not significantly visible.
>
> NGOs are playing a significant role in the society, but people in general are not aware of their work. People's perceptions about NGOs are also not correct. They are suspicious about NGOs and think that they have a concealed agenda. It is quite possible that there might be a few such NGOs as well but most of them are doing very productive work. For example, women's right associations all over Pakistan are doing very good work. They are working for the protection of women's rights. Similarly the Islamic Relief Fund is working for people's welfare in Afghanistan.
>
> I have worked with NGOs and they are doing very good work. They are creating significant awareness of environmental protection, noise pollution, hygiene and so on.

Why companies support NGOs

It is mostly large national companies that channel their support through NGOs. Various reasons were identified for this, as outlined below.

NGOS ARE MORE EFFECTIVE IN SOCIAL WELFARE WORK

Those who prefer to work through NGOs believe that their resources are utilized more effectively if channeled through NGOs because they have more experience and expertise in social welfare/development work. Moreover, they have networks for such work, which corporate companies lack.

COMPANIES DO NOT HAVE ENOUGH TIME TO BE DIRECTLY INVOLVED WITH END BENEFICIARIES

Time constraints were a major reason for some companies to support NGOs. These were large national companies, which tend to support long-term projects. They saw development work as a full-time job requiring specific expertise in terms of management and knowledge about communities' needs, so that supporting a credible NGO was the best option for supporting sustainable development.

'WE DO NOT HAVE ENOUGH RESOURCES TO MANAGE A SEPARATE DEPARTMENT FOR SOCIAL WELFARE/DEVELOPMENT WORK'

For some companies, due to the unavailability of sufficient resources to maintain a separate department for social work, it is more effective to work through NGOs.

NGOS CAN TAP INTO COMMUNITY RESOURCES THAT REDUCE THE TRANSACTION COST OF A PROJECT

Based on their own experience, some companies were of the view that since NGOs are working on a full-time basis, they have linkages and resources within different communities and are in a position to tap community resources, which reduces the transaction cost of projects. This adds to the resources given by the corporate sector and makes the project more effective and sustainable.

NGOS ARE BETTER PLATFORMS FOR MOBILIZING PEOPLE FOR PUBLIC CAUSES

Some organizations – though very few – were of the opinion that it is important to mobilize whole communities in order for community projects to be successful. Since only NGOs have the linkages for this, they are in the best position to mobilize community members and make it more likely that projects succeeded.

NGOS HAVE GREATER OUTREACH

Some companies were of the view that NGOs have greater outreach than corporate companies in communities throughout Pakistan, which better enables them to support disadvantaged communities. For example, commenting on this, one CEO stated:

> I think everything cannot be done by everyone. Therefore, we prefer to support NGOs that are doing better work. The main reason for us to support NGOs is that they have outreach in the far remote areas of the country, which we do not have and through them our resources are more effectively delivered to the ones who deserve them.

Companies' criteria for entering NGO partnerships

Companies were asked about their criteria for extending their support to NGOs. All companies supporting NGOs cited the credibility and transparency of NGOs (both administrative and financial) as the most important criteria. Second to credibility and transparency was the criterion of visibility. Around 21 per cent of organizations added NGOs' visibility in society as another criterion. For them, only NGOs that are visible have a good record of achievements.

Another important criterion mentioned was the vicinity of an NGOs' operations. If an NGO was working in a nearby area, it was more likely that the company would support that NGO. Eighteen per cent of companies preferred NGOs working in nearby areas. For almost all companies it was also important that the CEO or another senior official personally knew the NGO. Supporting NGO networks had lowest priority for almost all companies.

Length of partnership with NGOs

An important aspect of companies channelling support through NGOs was the length of their partnership. As shown in Figure 8.3, the data obtained from the survey reveals that the highest percentage of companies (74 per cent) channelled their support through NGOs on an annual basis. The ones providing support on a one-off basis made up 26 per cent and those providing support on an annual as well as a one-off basis 34 per cent.

Monitoring and evaluation

Monitoring is a key management tool to get information on project implementation and assess whether or not the project is moving towards its goals and objectives. Evaluation on the other hand is defined as an assessment of the defined activities and impact of a project. It is generally carried out at the end of the project, to determine its efficiency and efficacy.

Proper monitoring and evaluation also reflects the donor's outlook and concern about both the process and result of the project. In order to evaluate the extent to which corporate donors in Pakistan are concerned with the way their resources are used and the outcomes of their social involvement, the companies included in the survey were asked about their monitoring and evaluation tools.

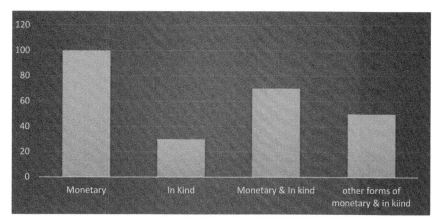

Figure 8.3 Different forms of support

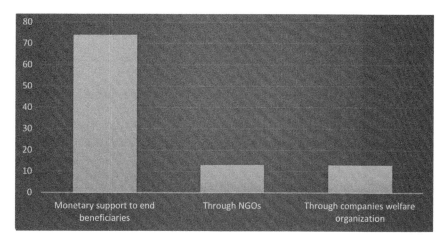

Figure 8.4 Stakeholders share of monetary support

As shown in Table 8.1, 43.7 per cent of companies do not monitor or evaluate their projects at all. However, of the 56.3 per cent of companies that do monitor and evaluate the projects they support, 0.7 per cent do so through monthly progress and financial reports, 4.6 per cent through quarterly progress and financial reports, 38.4 per cent through field visits, and 12.3 per cent through annual end evaluations.

The relationship between channels of support and companies' corporate social policies

There was an obvious correlation between companies' CSR policies and their channels of support. The percentage of companies channelling their support

Table 8.1 How do companies monitor and evaluate their NGOs and their own welfare organizations' projects?

Tools	Percentage
Monthly progress and financial reports	0.7
Quarterly progress and financial reports	4.6
Field visits	38.4
Annual evaluation of projects	11.3
No monitoring and evaluation	43.7
Total	100

Table 8.2 The correlation between channels of support and companies' CSR policies

	Percentage of companies	Written policy	Unwritten policy
Working directly with beneficiaries	95.4	12	88
Having their own welfare organizations	16.6	94	6
Working through an NGO	16.6	94	6

through NGOs or their own welfare organization and having a written CSR policy was significant. As indicated in Table 8.2, of the 16.6 per cent of companies channelling their support through NGOs, 94 per cent had a written CSR policy. Similarly, of the 16.6 per cent of companies channelling support through their own welfare organization, 94 per cent had a written CSR policy. On the other hand, of the 95.4 per cent of companies working directly with end beneficiaries, only 12 per cent had a written CSR policy. More importantly, most of the companies in that 12 percent belonged to the category of those channelling their support through NGOs as well as directly to end beneficiaries.

Forms of support

Different companies prefer to extend their support in different forms. Some prefer cash donations and some contribute in kind (non-monetary support); yet others prefer to offer their staff/CEOs as volunteers or provide technical support to end beneficiaries, NGOs or their own trust/welfare organizations.

Our survey asked respondents from various companies to provide information about their preferred forms of support when investing in the welfare/development sector. Three forms of support were identified:

1. Monetary support
2. Support in kind

3. Other forms of monetary and non-monetary support, including sponsorships, technical support and volunteering

As shown in Figure 8.3, all companies provided monetary support and 30 per cent provided support in kind. The companies that provided both monetary support and support in kind made up 70 per cent and those that provided other forms of monetary and non-monetary support comprised 49 per cent. In most cases, monetary support was provided on a one-off basis. This was especially true for small and medium-sized companies. The companies that provided in-kind support were mainly manufacturing companies that generally donated the products they produced themselves. During disasters, the percentage of in-kind support increases.

An analysis of companies' preferred forms of support and the reasons for providing support in those forms are given below.

Monetary support

According to our survey, 74 per cent of companies prefer extending monetary support to end beneficiaries, 13 per cent to NGOs, and another 13 per cent through the companies' own welfare organizations.

What CEOs consider when providing monetary support

There were several considerations identified when providing monetary support. These are described below.

THE CREDIBILITY OF THE PERSON/ORGANIZATION ASKING FOR SUPPORT AS WELL AS THAT OF THE CAUSE TO BE SUPPORTED

Whether it's an individual or an NGO asking for support, credibility was the most important consideration for almost all CEOs and other senior officials interviewed. For most companies, it was important that either the CEO himself or some of his senior officials already knew the persons/organizations when extending support.

The credibility of the cause was another consideration when providing monetary support. CEOs often had a view that when making cash donations, it was important for them to know that their contribution would go to the 'right' cause. The definition of 'right' cause varied from person to person. In general, it ranged from the purely religious cause to a mix of socio-religious causes for the wider public good. It was observed, however, that either knowledge of a certain cause or the emotional attachment of a CEO to a certain cause was the basic factor deciding the 'right' cause. Overall, except for a few cases, CEOs were not that rigid in sticking to a single cause. They were generally willing to support new causes introduced to them.

ASSOCIATION WITH PARTICULAR ISSUES

Whether for developing public goodwill, building the company image or some other purpose, it was found that a desire to be associated with particular issues was also an important consideration for companies when providing monetary support. For example, pharmaceutical companies often prefer to support health projects and banks extend their support to economic development projects.

AVAILABILITY OF FUNDS

Since monetary planning is an essential component of a successful business, no business invests even in their own business ventures unless the requisite funds are available. For corporate giving as well it was found from in-depth interviews of CEOs and other senior officials that the availability of funds was the primary concern when providing monetary support. This consideration was more important when making large donations than when making small donations to individuals.

SIZE OF DONATION REQUESTED

As mentioned above, the size of the donation requested is another important consideration in the decision whether to donate or not. Again, this is more relevant with larger amounts of money than with one-off small donations. In the case of larger donations, all the factors mentioned above – the credibility of the person/ organization asking for support, the availability of funds, etc. – become important.

PERSONAL WISHES OF THE CEO OR HIS FAMILY

In some cases, it was also found that the CEO invested in a cause because his family had a particular interested in making a cash donation.

Support in kind

Support in kind was the second best option for companies involved in welfare causes. Of the 30 per cent of companies that provided support in kind, 75 per cent provided support in kind directly to end beneficiaries and 25 per cent through NGOs or through companies' own welfare organizations (see Figure 8.5). However, during disasters, most in-kind support was channelled through NGOs. This is because NGOs working on disaster sites were able to reach the people in need.

Reasons for facilitating support in kind

IF MONEY WOULD NOT BE USEFUL

Most CEOs and senior officials stated that there are certain situations where support in kind is more appropriate than money. They cited instances of

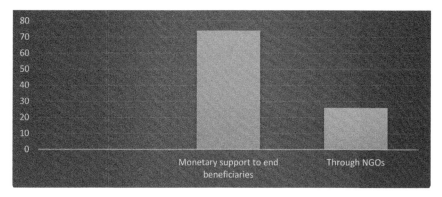

Figure 8.5 Per cent of in kind support directly of end beneficiaries and through NGOs

emergencies, floods and other natural and man-made disasters when they had extended support in kind. The items donated were food, blankets, tents, medicines and other items required for the relief of people in emergencies.

THE ITEMS DONATED ARE THE COMPANY'S OWN PRODUCTS

In general, the manufacturing companies preferred to donate their own products, this being more economic and convenient for them and also acting as a form of advertisement.

THE KIND OF ITEMS COMPANIES DONATE

The items companies donated ranged from food items, school equipment, clothing (both new and old), domestic appliances, computers, hospital equipment, medicines, dowry for poor girls, and sport equipments. As shown in Table 8.3, food items were the preferred form of in-kind donation, second being domestic appliances. Table 8.3 clearly reveals the everyday needs of poor people in Pakistan, who are not able to feed themselves adequately three times a day and lack clothing and domestic appliances.

Other forms of support

Apart from providing monetary and non-monetary support, the companies were also asked to indicate their involvement in the following forms of support:

- Sponsorships
- PR advertising
- Technical support
- Volunteering

In total, 50 per cent of companies provided other forms of support: 37 per cent provided sponsorships, 11 per cent invested in PR advertising for image-building,

Table 8.3 Items preferred for donation

Items	No.	Percentage
Food	123	42.12
School equipment	20	6.84
Clothing	52	17.8
Domestic appliances	67	22.94
Computers	2	0.68
Hospital equipment	23	7.87
Medicines	3	1.02
Dowry for poor girls	1	0.34
Sports equipment	1	0.34
Total	292	100

1 per cent provided technical support using company staff and 1 per cent provided volunteers.

Companies finance sponsorships for various purposes, including children's education, hospital rooms, clinics and madrassahs (religious schools), cultural and sporting events and religious causes. Excluding sponsorships for cultural and sporting events, the main motivation in most cases is religious.

Conclusions

The majority (95.4 per cent) of companies prefer to support end beneficiaries directly, while 16.6 per cent work through NGOs and 16.6 per cent through other intermediary organizations. The tendency to work directly with end beneficiaries rather than through some intermediary professional body highlights three important facts: 1) that corporate giving in Pakistan is still unorganized; 2) that the dominant mode of giving is philanthropic – Western-style CSR approaches have yet to be embedded in Pakistan, and 3) that NGOs have yet to play their role in creating awareness about the importance of organized CSR activities and yet to build their credibility.

Most CEOs had negative perceptions of NGOs and their main concern was NGOs credibility. Similarly, some were of the view that NGOs' administrative expenses are greater than the sum that reaches the end beneficiaries. Media – especially print media – and the negative propaganda campaigns of dissenters within the state and society, such as religious extremists accusing NGOs of being foreign agents working to some covert foreign agenda, seem to be propelling factors in creating negative perceptions of NGOs within the corporate sector. Many CEOs said that their perceptions of NGOs were not the outcome of any direct experience of working with them but because the mass media had developed a negative image of NGOs in their eyes. However, it is important to mention that the propaganda against NGOs from different sectors of society is also an outcome of the space that NGOs create for dissenters (mainly the government and religious segments) by their dependence on foreign funding and their lack of effort in establishing roots within society through local resource mobilization.

Local resource mobilization is not possible without social mobilization; when NGOs mobilize people for individual as well as for corporate support they develop their roots in society and build credibility. They cannot do this by relying only on foreign funding, which involves a different set of skills and mechanisms to acquire. Local resource mobilization is, therefore, not merely fundraising but 'friends-raising'. If NGOs have more friends they have more funds, because it is through friends that they can raise funds. A network of friends also helps establish an NGO's credibility.

More companies with written CSR policies channelled their support through NGOs than those found to be supporting end beneficiaries directly. The percentage of companies with written policies supporting NGOs was 21 per cent compared to 10 per cent supporting end beneficiaries directly. This indicates that a significant correlation exists between NGO partnerships and written CSR policies. Based on such a correlation, it can be argued that enhancing NGO-corporate sector partnerships can significantly advance the CSR movement in Pakistan.

The majority of companies (74 per cent) were found to be providing support to NGOs on an annual basis. The percentage of companies channelling their support on a one-off basis was 26 per cent and those opting for both was 34 per cent. This indicates that more partnerships with NGOs could be instrumental in generating more organized CSR activity.

Overall, the most widely preferred form of support was monetary support. The credibility and transparency of the individual or organizational cause was the most important criterion governing monetary as well as non-monetary support. Second to credibility was the availability of funds. Companies extending their support to society through NGOs or their own welfare organization mostly have a CSR policy. Manufacturing companies prefer in-kind support, donating their own products or, at times, providing them at a subsidized rate.

Note

1 Information on their projects/programmes is taken from their official websites: Hashoo Foundation: www.hashoofoundation.org/ (last accessed – 20 Jan 2014) and the Citizens Foundation: www.tcf.org.pk/ (last accessed – 20 Jan 2014).

9 Conclusions

The past decades have witnessed a significant shift in the influence over development policy and practice between three groups of global actors—governments, civil society and the corporate sector. Under the rubric of the 'good governance' paradigm advocating a lean state, the emergence of the corporate sector as one of the key drivers of development has become more apparent. Simultaneously, international agencies have taken the initiative to pressure companies to act in socially responsible ways. The UN Global Compact is the best known of these initiatives. Moreover, over the last decade we have also seen a shift from an overly critical view of the corporate sector by civil society to positive engagement between companies and civil society organizations.

The above is also a result of the development sector facing a new landscape with regard to resource mobilization for development in the face of diminishing foreign aid. The decline of foreign aid has been well entrenched globally since 1999. Competition for resources, therefore, has become a major feature of the NGO sector the world over. Several scholars therefore have talked about a 'beyond aid' scenario for development NGOs, emphasizing the need for local resource mobilization – of which tapping corporate resources for development is an important component.

In the context of state failure to deliver in developing countries such as Pakistan, the role of the corporate sector in development and the need for civil society to engage with the corporate sector becomes even more significant. Pakistan currently faces several challenges. These include: massive underdevelopment; decline in education, health and housing facilities; an uncontrollable law and order situation; the militarization of state and society; drug trafficking; ethnic and sectarian violence; child abuse and violence against women and minorities. On the economic front, the country is continuously in a state of dilapidation due to structural problems, a domestic energy crisis and decline in investment, persistent high inflation and security issues, and poverty is increasing, with 58.7 million of a total population of 180 million subsisting below the poverty line.

The state has failed to deliver in almost all important areas. This calls for enhanced efforts on part of civil society and the corporate sector to contribute significantly to the broader public good. The corporate sector especially has the essential resources to achieve this. Therefore, it seems only appropriate that this sector should play an active role in this area. It is already donating millions through philanthropic and charitable work. What is important is to organize corporate giving according to modern concepts of CSR.

Although in recent years awareness of this is becoming evident within the corporate sector in Pakistan, it still has a long way to go to achieve modern types of organized CSR activity. This is because of the underdevelopment of the industrial sector. The corporate sector has remained tied to family-orientated business concerns.

These family-orientated business concerns are the product of a kinship-based society where the corporate sector, because of the domination of families and their *biradari* networks, is unable to institutionalize according to modern norms and is resistent to innovation and radical reform. Such a social set-up gives birth to high power distance management systems with a hierarchical structure, where the father is considered head of the family and the eldest son has more say in decision-making than younger sons or sisters. In family businesses, unless the father retires he heads the organization, and if he retires, in most cases the eldest son succeeds him. Daughters, even if they are the eldest child, do not usually succeed the father as they are expected to eventually leave the parental home following marriage.

Such a state of affairs is reflected in the way CSR is managed. As mentioned earlier, though the contribution (both monetary and non-monetary) of the corporate sector in Pakistan is significant, in most cases it is essentially unorganized philanthropy and charitable in nature.

It is not surprising, therefore, that overall, only 41 (27.2 per cent) of the companies surveyed had a CSR policy, of which 63.4 per cent had a written and 36.6 per cent an unwritten (though formal) policy. It was mostly large national companies that had written policies. In most cases, the decision-making was centralized, with CEOs generally making the decisions regarding CSR. This was particularly pronounced in companies without a written CSR policy. This tendency was not restricted to decision-making: in a majority of companies, the CEO not only makes decisions about social investment activities but implements them as well.

The unorganized character of these CSR activities has important implications for the channels of support that companies opt for. The majority surveyed, 95.4 per cent, preferred to support end beneficiaries directly and 16.6 per cent preferred to channel their support through NGOs or other intermediary organizations. The support to end beneficiaries is charitable in nature. Some companies (16.6 per cent) were found to have their own intermediate bodies – welfare organizations and trusts – while others extended their support directly to end beneficiaries as well as through NGOs. This preference for working directly with end beneficiaries rather than through professional intermediary bodies highlights three important facts: 1) that corporate giving in Pakistan is still unorganized, 2) that the dominant mode of giving is philanthropic – Western-style CSR approaches have yet to be embedded in Pakistan – and 3) that NGOs have yet to engage the corporate sector and create awareness about the importance of organized CSR activities or build their credibility.

Most CEOs had negative perceptions of NGOs and their main concern was NGOs' credibility. Some were of the view that NGOs' administrative expenses are greater than the value of what reaches the end beneficiaries. in addition to the lack of significant engagement of development NGOs with the corporate sector, the media's negative campaigns and those of detracters within the state and society – such as religious extremists accusing NGOs of being foreign agents following some concealed foreign agenda – would appear to act as a propelling factor in creating these negative perceptions of NGOs. Many CEOs revealed that their perceptions of NGOs were not the result of any direct experience of working with them but arose from a mass media that does not project a positive image of NGOs. It is, however, important to mention that the propaganda against NGOs from different sections of society is also a result of the space that NGOs create for dissenters (e.g. the government, and religious segments of society) by solely depending on foreign funding.

Regarding priority areas for development, health and education were considered more important than areas such as the environment, women's rights, children's rights, water supply, sanitation, income generation and micro-credit. After the health sector, human rights was the next priority area of support. However, in most cases it was religious notions of rights that informed CEOs' views about human rights and as a result, some CEOs seemed conservative regarding women's rights, following their own interpretation of such rights according to Islam. Overall, it is difficult to conclude that their attitude to corporate giving was based on modern principles of development that take into account contemporary interpretations of human rights and involve the environment. Rather, it was to do with welfare. CSR was largely defined by CEOs as employee and community welfare, with a small percentage defining CSR as paying taxes.

The main motivation behind corporate giving was religious, rooted in the historical traditions of indigenous philanthropy/charity and community living. The chief reason for this is that though all religion encourage both philanthropy and charity, it has only been codified in Islam. Islam identifies four different forms of charity i.e. *Zakat, Zakat-al-Fitr, Khairat*, and *Sadaqa. Zakat* is one of the five pillars on which the religion is built. It is a way for those who have accumulated wealth to achieve salvation. According to Islam, when individuals fail to distribute *Zakat*, it is the responsibility of the state to collect and distribute it.

The other reason is that the Islamic religion has a bearing on the organizational culture in Pakistan, partly because, it is believed generally that the state of Pakistan emerged from the Islamic belief that Muslims on the Indian subcontinent were a separate nation due to their religion and their Islamic cultural heritage. Military rulers further strengthened this view – especially Zia-ul-Haq, who initiated a further phase of politically motivated extremist interpretations of Islam, the consequences of which are still visible in Pakistan.

Thus, for the reasons described above, CSR in Pakistan is still in its infancy. Only a few companies have a formal CSR strategy and mostly these are multinationals who follow their own CSR policies and standards. Some indigenous companies have written CSR policies, but the majority, unfortunately, are either unaware of the benefits of CSR or feel that they are not in any danger if they do not adopt such policies (Waheed 2005). In most cases, companies give charity to end beneficiaries, whether individuals or organizations, on a one-off basis. Religion, specifically Islam, provides a universal context for giving (whether individual or corporate) in Pakistan.

However, whatever the reasons (religion or kinship) behind CSR in Pakistan, it would be wrong to assume that modern CSR of the Western type can be imposed on the Pakistani cultural fabric. CSR has to evolve from that culture and its traditions. What would be worthwhile would be to create awareness within the corporate sector of the value of institutionalizing their CSR activities, so that their resources are not wasted on one-off philanthropic/charity work but can be used for long-term sustainable development. Civil society organizations and the government can play an important role in this regard. Both can create awareness about modern CSR through their engagement with the corporate sector.

An important role for the government is to control the black economy. Tax evasion, and the ubiquity of the black economy, has worked against proper financial reporting, which hinders CSR reporting as well. A lack of reporting becomes a disincentive to opt for written CSR policies or organized CSR activities. In this regard, the National Accountability Bureau strategy mentions the formalization and documentation of the economy and the need to develop integrity within the professions through the institutional strengthening of their regulatory mechanisms and ethics management, with a coalition of concerned professionals leading the way. Moreover, the State Bank of Pakistan has introduced a new regulatory framework related to financial responsibility and probity: Prudential Regulations for Corporate/Commercial Banking. The regulations require banks/development financial institutions (DFIs) to ensure that their business is conducted in conformity with high ethical standards and that the relevant laws and regulations are adhered to.

However, in societies such as Pakistan, where corruption and bad governance are pervasive, the tax-induced component of corruption cannot be overcome through strategies only but requires rigorous administrative measures and the stringent implementation of tax regulations. Thus, the tax administration responsible for the detection and tackling of tax evasion should be improved. The tax system must be simple, convenient and transparent. The system loopholes and prevailing corruption among tax collection authorities cannot be neglected and inefficiencies must be dealt with in order to curb tax evasion. Such measures could improve the overall quality of financial as well as CSR reporting.

Other initiatives by the public, private and NGO sectors could target any of the following:

1. Orientation and awareness
2. Changing perceptions
3. Developing joint ventures
4. Motivating company employees
5. Understanding and re-orientating corporate sector priorities
6. Building long-term relationships

Orientation and awareness

The orientation and awareness of both NGOs and the corporate sector regarding issues around corporate social responsibility is key to enhancing CSR for human development and overall economic growth and the attainment of basic human rights. The corporate sector is an important segment of society and, by making it part of a social development and human rights movement, civil society can develop a substantial support base for such issues. Similarly, the corporate sector can benefit through partnering with professional bodies and NGOs that have a better understanding of the needs of marginalized communities and better outreach. Through NGO partnerships, companies can also increase the impact of their social contribution through organized CSR activities. The government can also play an important role. It has taken some first steps. In July 2013, the SECP drafted Corporate Social Responsibility Guidelines. The basic objective of these guidelines is to promote the development of a framework for CSR initiatives by all companies. The government is encouraging companies to work in cooperation with stakeholders to implement a transparent and socially responsible business strategy. The guidelines suggest a CSR governance structure composed of the board of directors of the company committed to socially responsible business.

Overall, however, there is still a need for significant initiatives by the government, corporate sector and NGOs to create awareness about CSR in Pakistan. Below are some suggestions for action of this sort.

Seminars/conferences

1. A series of seminars needs to be organized on the subject of corporate social responsibility in all major cities in Pakistan. The seminars should explore all possible dimensions of CSR and its impact on society. Such seminars/conferences should eventually work towards the development of a national strategy and policy guidelines for the entire corporate sector in Pakistan to formalize their corporate social practices and, if possible, formulate written corporate social policies relating to their involvement in the development sector.

2. Seminars concerning 'rights-orientated' issues (human rights, women's rights, children's rights, etc.) need to be organized involving the corporate sector. The basic point that needs to be highlighted in such seminars is the connection between basic human rights and corporate social responsibility and the benefits the corporate sector can get from investing in human rights projects and supporting the human rights movement in Pakistan as the corporate sector does in developed countries.

Publications

More research and published materials are required to inform the government, civil society, the corporate sector and the whole society of the importance of CSR. A series of booklets in all the languages spoken in Pakistan needs to be published on the link between CSR, human development and rights-based approaches to development. Regarding rights-based approaches, such booklets would need to focus on three major aspects:

1. The relationship between corporate social responsibility and human rights, women's rights, children's rights, minority rights, etc.
2. The possible benefits to the corporate sector of investing in such projects.
3. Case studies of civil society organizations fighting for human rights, development and working for environmental issues in Pakistan.

Changing perceptions

The survey conducted clearly indicates the corporate sector's perceptions of NGOs in Pakistan. Although responses were mixed, both positive and negative, regarding the role and contribution of NGOs, it is important to address negative perceptions in an effective way. The following recommends action that could be taken to change such perceptions:

Involving media (both electronic and print) to initiate a debate on the issue of NGOs' successes and failures to achieve development/rights-based development and sustainable development in Pakistan. This should also include media visits to development sites where NGOs are working and short documentaries showcasing NGOs' efforts in development and human rights projects.

Developing joint ventures

Given that the government in Pakistan is so completely failing to provide the vast majority of its citizens with even the bare necessities, developing projects based on joint ventures of corporate and civil society institutions could be a very productive exercise. It would not only benefit society but also help develop an atmosphere of mutual trust and confidence between the corporate sector and civil society. Such projects would also be good examples for others to follow.

Motivating company employees

There are thousands of people working in the corporate sector, with numerous skills. Obtaining their participation could add significantly to civil society initiatives for development. It would be valuable to create an 'army' of supporters within the corporate sector to provide social and moral support regarding development and 'rights-orientated' issues in society. Companies need to be encouraged to introduce employees' voluntary programmes to participate in social development projects. To introduce such programmes companies could offer incentives to their employees in the form of awards and recognition. On the other hand, it is also the responsibility of civil society institutions to take the initiative to approach companies' employees directly or through company CEOs or senior staff and offer incentives for their involvement.

Understanding and re-orientating corporate sector priorities

Development NGOs can engage the corporate sector effectively if they are aware of companies' priorities areas for corporate support. This is only possible if tapping corporate resources becomes an important part of NGOs' resource mobilization strategy. The next step is to gradually create awareness within the corporate sector of what is actually needed by the various communities NGOs are working with in Pakistan. This would significantly help companies reconsider their priority areas as well as their outlook towards development and human rights in Pakistan.

Building long-term relationships

Once a relationship is established with a corporate sponsor, an NGO should take pains to turn this into a long-term partnership. NGOs must develop lasting bonds with businesses: too often, fund-raising is driven by the short-term need to make up a project's budget. This is not how major businesses treat each other, and it is not how NGOs should treat corporate benefactors. It is in the interest of both sides to become familiar with each other's potential on a broader basis.

As businesses start focusing on having definite policies for social investment, they will want to establish long-term relationships with reliable, effective NGOs who can become partners in addressing social, environmental and human rights concerns. NGOs should increasingly approach companies with a view to building a long-term relationship, one which will lead to 'repeat business' for the NGO. Even if a company has to turn down a proposal, it can help to find other corporate donors if the idea seem worthwhile.

References

Afghan, Nasir & Tayyaba, Wiqar (2007) 'Succession in family businesses of Pakistan: kinship culture and Islamic inheritance law', Centre for Management and Economic Research, Lahore University of Management Sciences.

AidWatch (2005) *Australian Aid: The Boomerang Effect*, Sydney: AidWatch.

Alavi, H. (1983) 'Class and state', in Gardezi, H. & Rashid, J. (eds) *Pakistan the Roots of Dictatorship: The Political Economy of a Praetorian State*, London: Zed Press.

Albareda, Laura, Lozano, Josep M. & Ysa, Tamyko (2007) 'Public policies on corporate social responsibility: the role governments in Europe', *Journal of Business Ethics*, Vol. 74, No. 4: 391–407.

Albareda, Laura, Lozano, Josep M., Tencati, Antonio, Midttun, Atle & Perrini, Francesco (2008) 'The changing role of governments in corporate social responsibility: drivers and responses', *Business Ethics: A European Review*, Vol. 17, No. 4: 347–63.

Aldaba, Fernando, Antezana, Paula, Valderrama, Mariano & Fowler, Alan (2000) 'NGO strategies beyond aid: perspectives from Central and South America and the Philippines', *Third World Quarterly*, Vol. 21, No. 4: 669–83.

Ali, Imran (1987) 'Malign growth? Agricultural colonization and the roots of backwardness in the Punjab', *Past & Present*, Vol. 114, No. 1: 110–32.

——(1988) *The Punjab under Imperialism, 1885–1947*, Princeton, NJ: Princeton University Press.

Ali, Imran & Malik, Adeel (2009) 'The political economy of industrial development in Pakistan: a long-term perspective', *Lahore Journal of Economics*, Vol. 14: 29–50.

——(2001) 'Business and power in Pakistan', in Weiss, Anita M. & Gilani, Zulfiqar S. *Power and Civil Society in Pakistan*, Karachi: Oxford University Press.

Ali, I., Rehman, K. U., Yilmaz, K. A., Nazir, S. & Ali, J. F. (2010) 'Effects of corporate social responsibility on consumer retention in cellular industry of Pakistan', *African Journal of Business Management*, Vol. 4, No. 4: 475–85.

Ali, Mubarak (1988) 'NGOs in Pakistan', in Jalalzai, M. K. (ed.) *The NGOs' Conspiracy in Pakistan*, Pakistan: Classic Publisher.

Ali, T. (2003) 'The color khaki', *New Left Review*, Vol. 19, Jan./Feb.

Alter, K. (2007) 'Social enterprise typology', *Virtue Ventures*. Available at www.virtueventures.com (accessed 10 April 2014).

Alvi, Anjum (2001) 'The category of the person in rural Punjab', *Social Anthropology*, Vol. 9, No. 1: 45–63.

Amalric, Franck, Kennedy-Glans, Donna, Reddy, Sanjay, O'Sullivan, Mary & Trevino, Javier (2004) 'Introduction: can CSR make a contribution to international solidarity and the quest for social justice in the South?' *Development*, Vol. 47, No. 3: 3–8.

Australian National Audit Office (ANAO) (2009) *AusAID's management of the expanding Australian Aid program*, Canberra: Australian National Audit Office.

Argenti, P. A. (2004) 'Collaborating with activists: How Starbucks works with NGOs', *California Management Review*, Vol. 47, No. 1: 91–116.

ARY News (2012) *Soch Pakistan*, 21 December.

Arshad, Mohammad Fayyaz (1989) 'Regional patterns of industrialisation in Pakistan', *Pakistan Economic and Social Review*, Vol. 27, No. 1: 17–31.

Atkinson D. & Claude, R. (2008) 'Human rights and multinational corporations: the Global Compact and continuing evolution', in Suder, G. (ed.) *International Business under Adversity*, Cheltenham: Edward Elgar.

Baber, Zaheer (2001) 'Modernization theory and the Cold War', *Journal of Contemporary Asia*, Vol. 31, No. 1.

Baig, Rabia & Sattar, Adnan (2001) 'Civil society in Pakistan: a preliminary report on the CIVICUS Index on Civil Society Project in Pakistan', *CIVICUS Index on Civil Society Occasional Paper Series*, Vol. 1, No. 11, NGO Resource Centre, Karachi.

Baig, Qadeer & Ismail, Zafar Hameed (2004) 'Philanthropy and law in Pakistan', *Philanthropy and Law in South Asia*. Available at http://asianphilanthropy.org/APPC/philanthropy-law-in-SouthAsia-2004.pdf (accessed 10 April 2014).

Banerjee, Abhijit Vinayak (2009) 'A capitalist knows who to call', in Kinsley, Michael & Clarke, Conor (eds) *Creative Capitalism: A Conversation with Bill Gates, Warren Buffett, and Other Economic Leaders*, New York: Simon & Schuster.

Basu, K. & Palazzo, G. (2008) 'Corporate social responsibility: a process model of sense making', *Academy of Management Review*, Vol. 33, No. 1: 122–36.

Bebbington, Anthony J. (1997) 'Reinventing NGOs and rethinking alternatives in the Andes', *The Annals of the American Academy of Political and Social Science*, Vol. 554, Nov.: 117–35.

Behn, S. (2013) 'Pakistan's 2012 human rights record bleak', *Voice of America*. Available at www.voanews.com/content/pakistan_2012_human_rights_record_is_bleak/1634992.html (accessed 10 April 2014).

Beurden, Van, Pieter & Gössling, Tobias (2008) 'The worth of values: a literature review on the relation between corporate social and financial performance', *Journal of Business Ethics*, Vol. 82, No. 2: 407–24.

Beyer, R. (1972) 'The "bottom line" is no longer, where it's at; an accounting executive lists five considerations for corporate social responsibility', *New York Times Magazine*, September 24.

Blowfield, Michael, & Frynas, Jedrzej George (2005) 'Editorial setting new agendas: critical perspectives on Corporate Social Responsibility in the developing world', *International Affairs*, Vol. 81, No. 3: 499–513.

Bonbright, David & Azfar, Asad (2000) *Philanthropy in Pakistan: a report of the initiative of indigenous philanthropy*, Pakistan: Agha Khan Foundation.

Bowen, H. R. (1953) *Social Responsibilities of the Businessman*, New York: Harper & Row.

Brammer, Stephen, Williams, Geoffrey & Zinkin, John (2007) 'Religion and attitudes to corporate social responsibility in a large cross-country sample', *Journal of Business Ethics*, Vol. 71, No. 3: 229–43.

Bremer, Jennifer (2004) 'Islamic philanthropy: reviving traditional forms for building social justice', paper presented at the CSID Fifth Annual Conference, Defining and Establishing Justice in Muslim Societies, Washington, DC, 28–29 May.

Bridges, Geoff (2007) *Asian Water Development Outlook 2007*, Asian Development Bank (ADB) Country Paper Pakistan: 9.

Brown, Duane & Brown, Gary D. (1975) *A Survey of the Social Sciences*, New York: McGraw-Hill Book Co.

Budhwar, P. (2001) 'HRM in India', in Budhwar, P. & Yaw, D. (eds) *HRM in Developing Countries*, London: Routledge.

Business Call to Action (2008) 'Business UN.org: partnering for a better world'. Available at www.businesscalltoaction.org/about/bcta-and-the-mdgs/ (accessed 18 May 2012).

Carroll, A. B. (1979) 'A three-dimensional conceptual model of corporate social performance', *Academy of Management Review*, Vol. 4, No. 4: 497–505.

——(1999) 'Corporate social responsibility: Evolution of a definitional construct', *Business and Society*, Vol. 38, No. 3: 268–95.

Carson, D. (1977) 'Point of view; companies as heroes? Bah! Humbug!!', *New York Times Magazine*, December 25.

Castello, I. & Lozano, J. (2011) 'Searching for new forms of legitimacy through corporate responsibility rhetoric', *Journal of Business Ethics*, Vol. 100, No. 1: 11–29.

Collier, P. (2007) *The Bottom Billion: Why the Poorest Countries Are Failing and What Can Be Done About It*, New York: Oxford University Press.

Dahlsrud, Alexander (2008) 'How corporate social responsibility is defined: an analysis of 37 definitions', *Corporate Social Responsibility and Environmental Management*, Vol. 15, No. 1: 1–13.

Daily Times (Pakistan) (2012) 'State of Pakistan economy: structural problems, energy crisis, others hinder growth', Staff Report, 15 April.

DAWN (2012) 'Poverty hovers around 33pc', *Daily DAWN*, Pakistan, 25 September.

——(2002) 'Compliance Initiative Board being set up', *Daily DAWN*, Pakistan, September 12.

DI (2012) 'Investments to end poverty: real money, real choices, real lives', *Development Initiatives*, Bristol.

Dreher, Axel, Mölders, Florian & Nunnenkamp, Peter (2007) 'Are NGOs the better donors? A case study of aid allocation for Sweden', *Kiel Working Papers* No. 1383, Kieler Arbeitspapiere.

Drucker, P. F. (1974) *Management: Tasks, Responsibilities, Practices*, New York: Harper & Row.

Drumwright, M. E. (1996) 'Company advertising with a social dimension: the role of non-academic criteria', *Journal of Marketing*, Vol. 60, No. 4: 71–86.

Dupuy, Kendra, Ron, James & Prakash, Aseem (2012) 'Foreign aid to local NGOs: good intentions, bad policy', *Open Democracy*. Available at www.opendemocracy.net/kendra-dupuy-james-ron-aseem-prakash/foreign-aid-to-local-ngos-good-intentions-bad-policy (accessed 10 April 2014).

Economic Watch (2003) *Poverty in Pakistan*, Saar Development Research Center, Lahore, Actionaid Pakistan.

Edwards, Michael, Hulme, David, & Wallace, Tina (1999) 'NGOs in a global future: marrying local delivery to worldwide leverage', *Public Administration and Development*, Vol. 19, No. 2: 117–36.

Escobar, Arturo (1995) *Encountering Development: The Making and Unmaking of the Third World*, Princeton, NJ: Princeton, University Press.

ESoP (2013) 'Population, labour force and employment', in *Economic Survey of Pakistan 2012–13*, Pakistan Bureau of Statistics, Government of Pakistan.

Esty, Daniel & Winston, Andrew (2009) *Green to Gold: How Smart Companies Use, Environmental Strategy to Innovate, Create Value, and Build Competitive Advantage*, Hoboken, NJ: John Wiley & Sons.

Farrington, J. & Lewis, D. (1993) *Non-Governmental Organisations and the State in Asia*, London: Routledge.

Fowler, Alan (1991) 'The role of NGOs in changing state–society relations: perspectives from Eastern and Southern Africa', *Development Policy Review*, Vol. 9, No. 1: 53–84.

——(2000) 'NGDOs as a moment in history: beyond aid to social entrepreneurship or civic innovation?' *Third World Quarterly*, Vol. 21, No. 4: 637–54.

Frances, Nic (2008) *The End of Charity-Time for Social Enterprise*, Crows Nest: Allen & Unwin.

Friedman, M. (1970) 'The social responsibility of business is to increase its profits', *Times Magazine*, New York, 13 September.

Frynas, Jedrzej George (2006) 'Introduction: corporate social responsibility in emerging economies', *Journal of Corporate Citizenship*, Vol. 6, No. 24: 16–19.

Frynas, Jedrzej George & Wood, Geoffrey (2001) 'Oil and war in Angola', *Review of African Political Economy*, Vol. 28, No. 90: 587–606.

Gardezi, H. (1983) 'Feudal and capitalist relations in Pakistan', in Gardezi, Hassan & Rashid, Jamil (eds) *Pakistan: The Roots of Dictatorship: the Political economy of a Praetorian State*, London: Zed Books.

Gardezi, Hassan & Rashid, Jamil (eds) (1983) *Pakistan: The Roots of Dictatorship: the Political Economy of a Praetorian State*, London: Zed Books.

Gideon, Jasmine (1998) 'The politics of social service provision through NGOs: a study of Latin America', *Bulletin of Latin American Research*, Vol. 17, No. 3: 303–21.

GoP (1949) *Economic Survey of Pakistan 1948–49*, Ministry of Finance, Government of Pakistan.

——(2004) *Medium Term Development Framework 2005–10. Section 10: Water and Sanitation*, Ministry of Planning and Development, Government of Pakistan.

——(2012) *Land Records Management and Information System*, Revenue Department, Government of Pakistan. Available at www.punjab-zameen.gov.pk/details.php?menuid=2&submenuid=8 (accessed 1 June 2012).

——(2013) *Growth and Investment, Economic Survey of Pakistan*, Government of Pakistan, Ministry of Finance.

Goyder, M. (2003) *Redefining CSR: From the Rhetoric of Accountability to the Reality of Earning Trust*, London: Tomorrow's Company.

Griffin, J. J. & Mahon, J. F. (1997) 'The corporate social performance and financial performance debate: twenty-five years of incomparable research', *Business and Society*, Vol. 36, No. 1: 5–31.

Guo, J., Sun, L. & Li, X. (2009) 'Corporate social responsibility assessment of Chinese corporation', *International Journal of Business Management*, Vol. 4, No. 4: 54–7.

Handler, W. C. (1994) 'Succession in family business: "a review of the research"', *Family Business Review*, Vol. 7, No. 2: 133–57.

Haq Mahbubul (1963) *Strategy of Economic Planning: A Case Study of Pakistan*, Oxford: Oxford University Press.

Hart, S. L. (1995) 'A natural-resource-based view of the firm', *Academy of Management Review*, Vol. 20, No. 4: 986–1014.

Henderson, D. (2001) *Misguided Virtue: False Notion of Corporate Social Responsibility*, Wellington: New Zealand Business Roundtable.

——(2004) *The Role of Business in the Modern World: Progress, Pressures and Prospects for the Market Economy*, London: Institute of Economic Affairs.

Hillman, A. J. & Keim, G. D. (2001) 'Shareholder value, stakeholder management and social issues: what's the bottom line?' *Strategic Management Journal*, Vol. 22, No. 2: 125–39.

Holloway, Richard (2001) *Towards Financial Self-Reliance*, London: Earthscan Publications.

HRCP (2010) *State of Human Rights in 2009*, Human Rights Commission of Pakistan.

——(2012) *State of Human Rights in 2011*, Human Rights Commission of Pakistan.

Ho, Virginia Harper (2013) 'Beyond regulation: a comparative look at state-centric corporate social responsibility and the law in China', *Vanderbilt Journal of Transnational Law*, Vol. 46, No. 2.

Hofstede, Geert (1983) 'The cultural relativity of organizational practices and theories', *Journal of International Business Studies*, Vol. 75, No. 89.

——(1991) *Cultures and Organizations: Software of the Mind*, London: McGraw-Hill.

Imaduddin (2013) 'Documentation of economy main focus of government', *Business Recorder*, 11 September.

Islam, Nasir (2004) 'Sifarish, sycophants, power and collectivism: administrative culture in Pakistan', *International Review of Administrative Sciences*, Vol. 70, No. 2: 311–30.

Ismail, Zafar H. (2002) 'Law and the non-profit sector in Pakistan', Social Policy and Development Centre, Working Paper No. 3, in collaboration with the Aga Khan Foundation (Pakistan) and the Center for Civil Society, Johns Hopkins University, USA.

Lipton, M. (1977) *Why Poor People Stay Poor: A Study of Urban Bias in World Development*, London: Temple Smith.

Lieven, Anatol (2011) *Pakistan: A Hard Country*, New York: Public Affairs.

Jalal, A. (1990) *The State of Martial Rule: The Origins of Pakistan's Political Economy of Defence*, Cambridge and New York: Cambridge University Press.

Jenkins, Rhys (2005) 'Globalization, corporate social responsibility and poverty', *International Affairs*, Vol. 81, No. 3: 525–40.

Jhatial, Ashique Ali, Mangi, Riaz Ahmed & Ghumro, Ikhtiar Ali (2012) 'Antecedents and consequences of employee turnover: empirical evidence from Pakistan', *British Journal of Management & Economics*, Vol. 2, No. 4: 279.

Jilani, H. (1998) 'Human rights and democratic development in Pakistan' Lahore: Human Rights Commission of Pakistan.

Johnson, R. D. & Greening D. W. (1999) 'The effects of corporate governance and institutional ownership types on corporate social performance', *Academy of Management Journal*, Vol. 42: 564–76.

Judge, W. Q. & Douglas, T. J. (1998) 'Performance implications of incorporating natural environmental issues into the strategic planning process: an empirical assessment', *Journal of Management Studies*, Vol. 35, No. 2: 241–60.

Kanungo, R. & Mendonca, M. (1994) 'Culture and performance improvement', *Productivity*, Vol. 35, No. 4: 447–53.

Karabulut, A. Tugba & Demir, Oguz (2006) 'The rising trend for NGO and the private sector cooperation: corporate social responsibility', *Journal of Turkish Weekly*. Available at www.turkishweekly.net/article/160/the-rising-trend-for-ngo-and-the-private-sec tor-cooperation-corporate-social-responsibility.html (accessed 10 April 2014).

Khan, Foquie Sadiq & Nomani, Uzma (2002) 'Corporate social responsibility and natural disaster reduction in Pakistan', Sustainable Development Policy Institute, Islamabad, Pakistan.

Khan, Mushtaq H. (1999) 'The Political Economy of Industrial Policy in Pakistan 1947–1971', SOAS Department of Economics Working Paper No. 98, University of London.

Khan, Rabia Mansoor (2013) 'Relationship between financial performance and CSR activities in companies in Pakistan', *Interdisciplinary Journal of Contemporary Research in Business*, Vol. 4, No 10: 918–28.

Khilji, Shaista E. (2003) 'To adapt or not to adapt: exploring the role of national culture in HRM: a study of Pakistan', *International Journal of Cross-Cultural Management*, Vol. 3, No. 1: 109–32.

Kitchin, T. (2002) 'Corporate social responsibility: a brand explanation', *Brand Management*, Vol. 10, No. 4/5: 312–26.

Klassen R. D. & McLaughlin, C. P. (1996) 'The impact of environmental management on firm performance', *Management Science*, Vol. 42, No. 8: 1199–214.

Kochanek, Stanley A. (1983) *Interest Groups and Development: Business and Politics in Pakistan*, Karachi: Oxford University Press.

Koestoer, Yanti T. (2007) 'Corporate social responsibility in Indonesia: building internal corporate values to address challenges in CSR implementation', Seminar on Good Corporate and Social Governance in Promoting ASEAN's Regional Integration. Jakarta: ASEAN Secretariat.

Korten, D. C. (2001) *When Corporations Rule the World*, Bloomfield, CT: Berrett-Koehler Publishers.

Kostova, T. & Zaheer, S. (1999) 'Organizational Legitimacy Under Conditions of Complexity: The Case of the Multinational Enterprise', *Academy of Management Review*, Vol. 24, No. 1: 64–81.

Kosambi, D. D. (1975) *An Introduction to the Study of Indian History*, Bombay: Popular Prakashan.

Kshetri, Nir (2011) 'Emerging economies and the global financial crisis: evidence from China and India', *Thunderbird International Business Review*, Vol. 53, No. 2: 247–62.

Lantos, G. P. (2001) 'The boundaries of strategic corporate social responsibility', *Journal of Consumer Marketing*, Vol. 18, No. 2: 595–630.

——(2003) 'Corporate socialism masquerades as "CSR": the difference between being ethical, altruistic and strategic in business', *Strategic Direction*, Vol. 19, No. 6: 31–5.

Lee, Min Dong Paul (2008) 'A review of the theories of corporate social responsibility: Its evolutionary path and the road ahead', *International Journal of Management Reviews*, Vol. 10, No. 1: 53–73.

Leftwich, Adrian (1995) 'Bringing politics back in: towards a model of the developmental state', *Journal of Development Studies*, Vol. 31, No. 3: 400–27.

Longenecker, J. G. & Schoen, J. E. (1978) 'Management Succession in the Family Business', *Journal of Small Business Management*, Vol. 16, No. 3: 1–6.

Lyon, Stephen M. (2004) *An Anthropological Analysis of Local Politics and Patronage in a Pakistani Village*, New York: Edwin Mellen Press.

Mahmood, Babak (2008) 'Sociological study of behavioral change in textile manufacturing organizations of Punjab, Pakistan: in context of global business culture', dissertation, University of Agriculture, Pakistan.

Malik, Nadeem (2001) *Tapping Local Resources*, Karachi: City Press.

——(2009) *Citizens and Governance in Pakistan: An Analysis of People's Voices*, Lahore: Sanjh Publications.

——(2011) 'Development studies: discipline or interdisciplinary field?' in Rashid, T. & Flanagan, J. (eds) *International Development: Linking Academia with Development Aid and Effectiveness*, Koln: Lambert Academic Publishing, pp. 13–27.

Malhotra, Kamal (2000) 'NGOs without aid: beyond the global soup kitchen', *Third World Quarterly*, Vol. 21, No. 4: 655–8.

Manne, G. H. (1972) 'Responsibility: social role of business could lead to market's extinction', *New York Times Magazine*, February 20.

Manne, H. G. & Wallich, H. C. (1972) *The Modern Corporation and Social Responsibility*, Washington, DC: American Enterprise Institute for Public Policy Research.

Margolis, J. D. & James P. W. (2001) *People and Profits? The Search for a Link between a Company's Social and Financial Performance*, Mahwah, NJ: Erlbaum.

McLeod, Heather, (1997) 'Cross over: the social entrepreneur', in *Inc. Special Issue: State of Small*, Vol. 19, No. 7: 100–4.

Manokha, I. (2004) 'Corporate social responsibility: a new signifier? An analysis of business ethics and good business practice', *Politics*, Vol. 24, No. 1: 56–64.

Mercer, Claire (2002) 'NGOs, civil society and democratization: a critical review of the literature', *Progress in Development Studies*, Vol. 2, No. 1: 5–22.

Mintzberg H. (1983) 'The case for corporate social responsibility', *Journal of Business Strategy*, Vol. 4, No. 2: 3–15.

Mogens, Buch-Hansen & Lauridsen, Laurids S. (2012) 'The past, present and future of development studies', *Forum for Development Studies*, Vol. 39, No. 3.

Moore, G. (2003) 'Hives and horseshoes, Mintzberg and McIntyre: what future for corporate social responsibility?' *Business Ethics: a European Review*, Vol. 12, No. 1: 41–53.

Morton, Bill (2013) 'An overview of international NGOs in international development cooperation', Case Study 7, in *Working for Civil Society in Foreign Aid*, UNDP China.

National Accountability Bureau (NAB) (2002) 'National anti-corruption strategy', National Accountability Bureau, Government of Pakistan.

Nadeem, A. H. (1970) 'Growth of industries in the public sector: a case study of Pakistan', *The Punjab University Economist*, Vol. 8, No. 1: 7–22.

Naeem, Malik Asghar & Welford, Richard (2009) 'A comparative study of corporate social responsibility in Bangladesh and Pakistan', *Corporate Social Responsibility and Environmental Management*, Vol. 16, No. 2: 108–22.

Nazir, Mian Sajid (2009) 'Corporate social disclosure in Pakistan: a case study of the fertilizer industry', *Journal of Commerce*, Vol. 2, No. 1: 1–11.

Nishat, Mohammed (2013) 'The economic impacts of inadequate sanitation in Pakistan', Water and Sanitation Programme, Islamabad, Pakistan

O'Riordan, Linda & Fairbrass, Jenny (2008) 'Corporate social responsibility (CSR): models and theories in stakeholder dialogue', *Journal of Business Ethics*, Vol. 83, No. 4: 745–58

Pakistan Market Profile (2014) 'Microfinance in Pakistan', Washington, DC: MIX Market. Available at www.mixmarket.org/mfi/country/Pakistan?gclid=CLPU2enh 2r0CFUUGvAodxWwAHw (accessed 10 April 2014).

Pakistan Defense (2012) 'Global literacy rate: Pakistan ranks 113th among 120 nations'. Available at http://defence.pk/threads/global-literacy-rate-pakistan-ranks-113th-among-120-nations.215159/.

Palazzo, G. & Scherer, A. (2006) 'Corporative legitimacy as deliberation: a communicative framework', *Journal of Business Ethics*, Vol. 66, No. 1: 71–88.

PBS (2013) *Household Integrated Economic Survey (HIES)*, Pakistan Bureau of Statistics, Government of Pakistan.

Peloza, J. (2006) 'Using corporate social responsibility as insurance for financial performance', *California Management Review*, Vol. 48, No. 2: 52–72.

Power, John H. (1963) 'Industrialization in Pakistan: a case of frustrated take-off?' *The Pakistan Development Review*, Vol. 3, No. 2: 191–207.

Prahalad, C. (2005) *The Fortune at the Bottom of the Pyramid*, Upper Saddle River, NJ: Wharton School Publishing.

Qureshi, Saeed Ahmed (2000) 'The meaning of philanthropy', *Business Recorder*, Pakistan, 16 October.

Rana, Javed (2013) 'Pakistan's thriving black economy hits $9.5 billion', *Dateline Islamabad*, 16 September.

Rashid, Amjad   (2009) 'Pakistan on the brink', *New York Review of Books*, June 11.

——(1983) 'Industrial concentration and economic power', in Gardezi, H. & Rashid, J. (eds) *Pakistan the Roots of Dictatorship: The Political Economy of a Praetorian State*, London: Zed Books.

Rauf, Abdur (1983) 'Education and development', in Gardezi Hassan & Rashid Jamil (eds) *Pakistan: The Roots of Dictatorship: the Political Economy of a Praetorian State*, London: Zed Books.

Ravallion, M. & Chen, S. (2009) 'The developing world Is poorer than we thought, but no less successful in the fight against poverty', *Policy Research Working Paper Series*, No. 4703, World Bank Research Development Group.

Rehnema, Majid (1991) 'Global poverty: a pauperizing myth', *Interculture*, Vol. 24, No. 2: 4–51.

Reis, Tom (1999) *Unleashing the New Resources and Entrepreneurship for the Common Good: a Scan, Synthesis and Scenario for Action*, Battle Creek, MI: W. K. Kellogg Foundation.

Rondinelli, Dennis A. & Berry, Michael A. (2000) 'Environmental citizenship in multinational corporations: social responsibility and sustainable development', *European Management Journal*, Vol. 18, No. 1: 70–84.

Sachs, Wolfgang (1990) 'The archaeology of the development idea', *Interculture*, Vol. 23, No. 1: 1–37.

SBP (2011) 'Prudential regulations for corporate/commercial banking', Banking Policy and Regulations Department, State Bank of Pakistan.

SDPI (2012) 'Increasing level of poverty in Pakistan', Sustainable Development Policy Institute (SDPI), Islamabad, Pakistan.

Securities and Exchange Commission of Pakistan (SECP) (2013) 'Corporate Social Responsibility Guidelines 2013', Security and Exchange Commission, Government of Pakistan.

Seljuq, Affan (2005) 'Philanthropy and charity in Pakistan,' *Journal of Management and Social Sciences*, Vol. 1, No. 1: 85–98.

Sen, Amartya (1999) *Development as Freedom*, Oxford: Oxford University Press.

Sarmila, M. S., Zaimah, R., Lyndon, N., Azima A. M., Saad, Suhana & Selvadurai, S. (2013) 'The roles of government agency in assisting CSR project for community development: analysis from the recipients' perspectives', *Asian Social Science*, Vol. 9, No. 8: 17–22.

Sharma, P., Chrisman, J. J., and Chua, J. H. (2003) 'Succession planning as planned behavior: some empirical results', *Family Business Review*, Vol. 16, No. 1: 1–15.

Simons, A. & Tucker, D. (2007) 'The misleading problem of failed states: a socio-geography of terrorism in the post-9/11 era', *Third World Quarterly*, Vol. 28, No. 2: 387–401.

Smith, N. Craig (2003) 'Corporate social responsibility: not whether, but how', London Business School/Centre for Marketing Working Paper 03–701.

Somjee, A. H. (1984) *Political Society in Developing Countries*, London: Macmillan Press.

Syed, M. A. (2013) 'The state, donors and poor Pakistani farmers in Sindh and Punjab', PhD dissertation, School of Social and Political Sciences, University of Melbourne.

Spector, Bert (2008) 'Business responsibilities in a divided world: the Cold War roots of the corporate social responsibility movement', *Enterprise and Society*, Vol. 9, No. 2: 314–36.

Talbot, Ian (2009) *Pakistan: A Modern History*, London: Hurst & Co.

Tayeb, Monir (1995) 'The competitive advantage of nations: the role of HRM and its socio-cultural context', *International Journal of Human Resource Management*, Vol. 6, No. 3: 588–605.

——(1997) 'Islamic revival in Asia and HRM', *Employee Relations*, Vol. 19, No. 4: 352–64.

——(2001) 'Conducting research across cultures', *International Journal of Cross-cultural Management*, Vol. 1, No. 1: 91–108.

Tearle, F. J. E (1965) 'Industrial development in Pakistan', *Journal of the Royal Central Asian Society*, Vol. 52, No. 3/4: 224–37.

UN Global Compact (2012) 'Overview of the UN Global Compact'. Available at www.unglobalcompact.org/AboutTheGC/index.html (accessed 10 April 2014).

Waddock, S. A. & Samuel, B. G. (1997) 'The corporation social performance-financial performance link', *Strategic Management Journal*, Vol. 18, No. 4: 303–19.

Waheed, Ambreen (2005) *Evaluation of the State of Corporate Social Responsibility in Pakistan and a Strategy for Implementation*, Securities & Exchange Commission of Pakistan and United Nations Development Program.

Waseem, Mohammad (1994) *The 1993 Elections in Pakistan*, Lahore: Vanguard.

Weekly Independent (2005) *Managing Karachi's water supply and sanitation services: lessons from a workshop*, Lahore, March 17.

Wiarda, Howard J. & Boilard, Steven (1999) 'Introduction', in Wiarda, Howard J. (ed.) *Nonwestern Theories of Development: Regional Norms versus Global Trends*, Fort Worth, TX: Harcourt Brace College.

Wales, A., Gorman, M. & Hope, D. (2010) *Big Business, Big Responsibilities: From Villains to Visionaries: How Companies are Tackling the World's Greatest Challenges*, Basingstoke: Palgrave Macmillan.

Wan Jan, W. S. (2006) 'Defining corporate social responsibility', *Journal of Public Affairs*, Vol. 6, No. 34: 176–84.

Warden, S. (2007) 'Joining the fight against global poverty: a menu for corporate engagement', Washington, DC: Centre for Global Development.

Wilson, C. & Wilson, P. (2006) *Make Poverty Business: Increase Profits and Reduce Risks by Engaging with the Poor*, Sheffield: Greenleaf Publishing.

Wise, Victoria & Ali, Muhammad Mahboob (2008) 'Case studies on corporate governance and corporate social responsibility', *South Asian Journal of Management*, Vol. 15, No. 3: 136–49.

World Bank (2011) *Bangladesh at a Glance*, Washington, DC: The World Bank. Available at http://devdata.worldbank.org/AAG/bgd_aag.pdf (accessed 3 April 2011).

——(2011b) *The Economic Impacts of Inadequate Sanitation in Pakistan*, Washington DC: World Bank. Available at http://documents.worldbank.org/curated/en/2011/01/16232510/economic-impacts-inadequate-sanitation-pakistan (accessed 10 April 2014).

Young, N. (2002) 'Three "C"s: Civil society, corporate social responsibility and China', *The China Business Review*, Vol. 29, No. 1: 34–8.

Zaidi, Akbar S. (1999) 'Institutional failure, state failure or the failure of "civil" society? The rural water supply and sanitation sector in Pakistan', *Lahore Journal of Economics*, Vol. 5, No. 2: 71–90.

Zulkifi, Norhayh & Azlan, Amran (2006) 'Realising corporate social responsibility in Malaysia', *Journal of Corporate Citizenship*, Vol. 24: 101–14.

Index

For Product Safety Concerns and Information please contact our EU
representative GPSR@taylorandfrancis.com Taylor & Francis Verlag GmbH,
Kaufingerstraße 24, 80331 München, Germany

Printed and bound by CPI Group (UK) Ltd, Croydon, CR0 4YY
08/05/2025
01864386-0001